SILK
PAINTING
Techniques and Ideas

SILK PAINTING

Techniques and Ideas

Jill Kennedy

Jane Varrall

B. T. BATSFORD

First published 1991

Typeset by Keyspools Ltd, Golborne, Lancs
and printed in Hong Kong

Published by B. T. Batsford Ltd
4 Fitzhardinge Street, London W1H 0AH

ISBN 0 7134 6481 X

A catalogue record for this book is available from the British Library

Acknowledgements

We would like to thank our husbands and our families for their continued support and encouragement. We would also like to thank Catherine for typing, Sarah and Jean-Pierre.

Photographs
J. P. Van Den Wayenberg
Fotostudio Jean-Pierre
Mechelsesteenweg 232
1960 Sterrebeek
Belgium

CONTENTS

INTRODUCTION

If you, like many others, have recently become interested in the art of painting on silk, you may have asked yourself this question: having produced a beautiful design on a beautiful material, what are you going to do with it? This book will help by giving practical advice on how to make the most of the opportunities silk painting offers to create your own clothes, accessories, furnishings and decorations.

The first section is a brief but comprehensive description of the equipment and techniques used in silk painting. The main body of the book, however, comprises the 'projects' and has been organized into three sections: fashions, home furnishings and accessories. (We are using this last term as a 'catch-all' to cover everything from jewellery to Christmas decorations, and we hope you will find a few novel ideas here!)

You should be able to achieve professional-looking results by following the detailed instructions and diagrams on planning, sewing or finishing any of the projects. We have used as many pictures as possible to help you envisage the finished articles, and to illustrate some of the methods. Scale drawings are included for the reader who lacks the confidence to 'design', but we hope that the original work we have shown will stimulate your imagination and creativity.

PART ONE

TOOLS and MATERIALS

EQUIPMENT

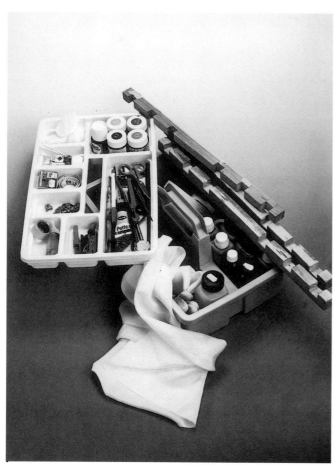

Silk painting equipment

To begin painting on silk, you will need the following:

- Silk
- Frames, pins
- Brushes and applicators
- Gutta
- Wax
- Salt, sugar, alcohol
- Dyes and thinning agents
- Scissors, pencil, masking tape, cotton wool, tracing, graph and drawing paper, hair dryer

Silk

Silk is a superb fabric to work with and can be used for all the projects shown in this book. It can be woven in various ways to produce fabric of different types and textures. The following types can all be used for the projects described in this book:

pongée no. 5–10 (habutai or jap silk)

twill

wild (raw or tussah, soie sauvage)

crêpe de Chine

brocade

chiffon

satin

shantung

organza

taffeta

Pongée no. 9

Pongée or habutai, a lightweight lining material, is most commonly used for silk painting and can usually be found in your local department store or fabric shop. This lightweight silk is ideal for the beginner as the dyes flow easily and gutta penetrates the fibres creating a fast barrier. Smooth and shiny, it is an ideal fabric; it is sold in a variety of thicknesses from nos 5 to 10: the higher the number, the thicker the silk. It also has the advantage of being the cheapest silk available. Choose white silk initially as the dyes will show up in their true colours. If you choose cream, beige or any other colours you must test your dyes on a sample to check the end results. Pongée no. 5 is very good for experimental techniques such as salt, alcohol and watercolour, mainly because it is less expensive, but also because the dyes react well on the fine fabric. No. 9 we find is the most useful as it works well for scarves, lampshades and pictures; no. 10 can be used for cushions, ties, blouses and fashion projects.

Wild or raw silk is much thicker and more textured and is ideal for ties, jackets, blouses and cushion covers.

Crêpe de Chine drapes and hangs beautifully and makes wonderful clothes and exclusive scarves. **Brocade** and **satin** are also favourites for lingerie and clothes.

Caring for your silk

It is advisable to clean the silk before painting, to remove any dressing; some silks may have had an application of size to increase their weight. Before painting, wash the silk thoroughly in warm soapy water, rinse in warm water and roll in a tea towel to remove excess moisture. Iron with a steam iron while still damp. The dyes will then penetrate the fibres evenly and thoroughly. Also use this method when washing a finished article; do not use a harsh detergent, as it may cause the colours to fade.

Frames

A wooden frame is an essential piece of equipment when painting on silk. The fabric must be raised above the work surface, so it is necessary for it to be stretched taut over a rigid frame. There are several types of frame available: fixed, sliding and adjustable. The fixed wooden frame is easy to make: just cut four lengths of

Fixed, adjustable slot and sliding frames

9

soft wood to the required size and fix together with butt or mitred joints. An old picture frame could be used. The adjustable wooden slot frame or sliding frames are very useful as they can be used for various sizes of fabric. We have found that the soft wood adjustable frame which accommodates a 90 cm × 90 cm (36 in × 36 in) fabric is the most useful; many projects of different sizes can be painted using this frame.

When working with a large piece of silk which needs to be painted in one piece, for example a kimono or sarong, it is a good idea to improvise a frame by securing two planks of soft wood between two wooden trestles, or to join two adjustable wooden slot frames end to end. If, however, you intend to paint a lot of large scarves or sarongs of the same size, it may be worth your while to buy a large sliding frame; or make a frame 150 cm × 90 cm (60 in × 36 in), or the size you will need for your chosen project.

Pins

To stretch the silk you need special fine pointed pins which will not tear the silk when it is secured to the frame. Architect's pins are ideal, as they have three small points which hold the silk firmly on the frame. They can be removed easily by using a small lever. If you cannot find these, look for push pins or drawing pins with long fine points.

Stretching silk on a frame

Before stretching the silk on the frame it is a good idea to protect the frame by covering the top surface with masking tape. This tape may become dye stained but can easily be removed and renewed before each project. Place the silk design side uppermost and begin pinning along one side, following the grain of the fabric. Some people prefer to place pins in all four corners or start in the middle of each side. Whichever method you choose, be sure to stretch the silk tightly using the grain of the fabric as a guide. When you have finished pinning, the silk should be as tight and firm as a drum.

Masking the frame with tape

Silk being stretched on the frame

Firmly stretched silk

Brushes

A selection of silk painting brushes, wax brushes and applicators

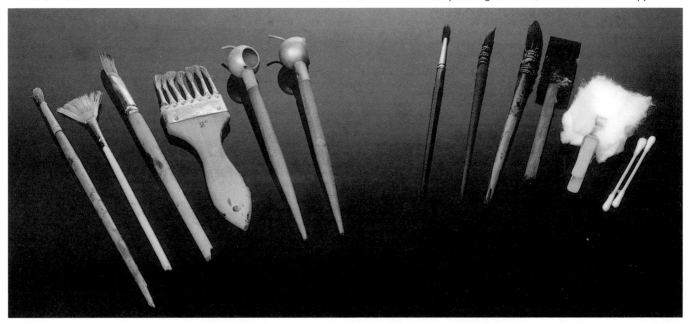

There are many types of brush available, but you can manage with just three brushes of different sizes. Wash brushes and specialized silk painting brushes are ideal. Depending on their size, they are able to hold enough dye to cover large areas. Cottonwool can be used as an alternative, and foam pads are handy when covering large areas. Brushes are expensive, so take great care of them. Never leave them soaking for long periods in water and store them with their tips uppermost.

Gutta

Gutta or resist is the liquid you use to transfer the outline of the design to the silk. There are two types of gutta: rubber based, which can be diluted by a solvent, and water-soluble. When the gutta penetrates fibres of the silk it creates a barrier which is waterproof and therefore dyeproof. After the gutta line has been applied to the silk it remains soft and pliable, even when it has dried. The colour of the silk will show through the gutta lines, unless of course you are using a metallic or coloured gutta.

Coloured gutta is usually sold in smaller containers and is more expensive. It is possible to make your own coloured gutta by adding stained glass colour or typographic ink to the colourless variety. To prepare this, mix a small amount of colour with the solvent and then add to the colourless gutta. Coloured and metallic guttas should not be dry cleaned, as this dissolves the colour.

Preparation of gutta

The consistency of the gutta is very important: if it is too thick or too thin it will not create a fast barrier and the dye will flow over or under the gutta line. It is possible to thin down the gutta, if it has become thick and sticky, by using one of several thinning agents, depending on the type of gutta you are using. The gutta must be diluted using the solvent the manufacturer suggests on the bottle, lighter fuel or white spirit. If you add too much solvent by mistake, leave the bottle open for a while and some of the solvent will evaporate. Always do a small sample to check the gutta and dyes.

Pipettes, gutta and nibs

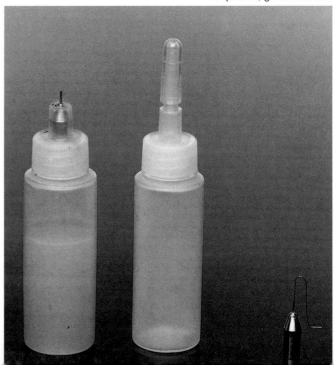

Containers for the application of gutta

To draw the gutta line a pipette or cone is needed (see opposite, below). It is much easier to use a pipette, which is a small plastic bottle with a long spout. To fill the pipette, remove the screw top and spout and slowly pour the gutta into the bottle. The plastic spout can be pierced with a fine needle, but the best way is to affix a nomographic nib (metal-tipped spout) which produces a perfect, even line. These nibs are available in sizes from nos 4 to 10 (the lower the number, the finer the hole). We suggest a no. 5 or no. 6 unless a very thick line is required, when a no. 9 or no. 10 should be used. The nib can be secured to the plastic spout with tape or placed inside the screw-on top after cutting off the plastic spout. To keep nibs clean they should be placed in an airtight container of thinning fluid after use. Gutta will start to harden if left out overnight, so drain any remaining solution back into the original bottle.

Wax

Hot wax can be used in the same way as gutta (see pages 24 and 25). When applied to the silk it creates a barrier to any dye by penetrating the fibres. This process of applying molten wax and dyes is traditionally known as batik. We will explain a method called false batik which will enable you to create exciting and original results. The wax used is a mixture of paraffin wax and beeswax. These can be obtained from hardware stores, craft shops or candlemakers' suppliers.

Heating wax

The wax must be heated slowly. This can be done by one of the following methods: a thermostatically controlled wax pot, an electric ring or a gas burner with a double boiler, saucepan or aluminium tin.

When melted, the wax is applied to the silk. If it is the correct temperature, it will leave a transparent line. If the wax sits on the surface of the silk and looks white, it has not penetrated and the dyes will flow under it. If the wax is too hot, it will spread too far and the brushes will burn.

Equipment for the application of wax

Brushes of any size and shape can be used to apply wax. The brushes can be cleaned in white spirit, but it is best to reserve a few brushes for wax use only. Tjantings can also be used. A tjanting is a small copper bowl attached to a wooden handle with one or more spouts. It is dipped into the hot wax to fill the copper bowl and then the molten wax is applied to the fabric through the spout.

Wax pot, wax and candles

Salt, sugar and alcohol

Salt, sugar and alcohol can be used to create different and exciting textures when used in conjunction with silk painting dyes (see pages 26 and 27). Medicinal alcohol, methylated spirits and surgical spirit can all be used and are available from chemists or hardware shops. Salt is available in several qualities: fine table salt, sea salt, dishwater salt and rock salt. These all produce different unusual textures. Sugar can also be used, either white granulated or icing sugar.

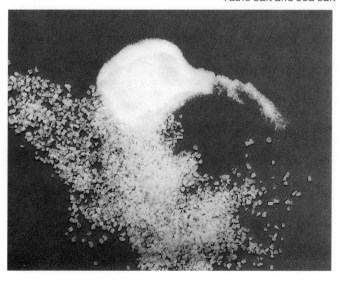

Table salt and sea salt

Dyes

There are many silk-painting dyes now on the market. We have placed them into three categories, depending on their method of fixing. Check the manufactuer's instructions. These should be clearly marked on whichever brand of dye you buy.

Dyes, palette and markers

Steam-fixed dyes

These are transparent and penetrate the material thoroughly. It is fun to experiment superimposing one colour over another while the first colour is still wet. The brightness and permanence of colour is excellent, and once fixed by steam the silk is washable and dry cleanable. These dyes are non-toxic and odourless. They are available at art and craft shops under a variety of brand names. Pastel-type silk painting crayons can be used to sketch and draw on the silk. These also need to be fixed by steam.

Heat-fixed dyes

These are thicker and less transparent than the steam-fixed dyes. They do not penetrate the fibres of the silk completely unless watered right down and therefore the reverse of the design may not be as clear and bright as the front. The great advantage of these dyes is their easy fixing method using a hot iron. There are many types, available under a variety of brand names. Once fixed, these dyes are washable and dry cleanable.

Special dye-filled pens with felt tips are also available to draw on silk, and these are great for children.

Liquid-fixed dyes

These dyes are water-based and are fixed using a liquid fixer. They are non-toxic and after fixing are washable and dry cleanable.

Mixing the dyes

All of the dyes are available in a wide range of vibrant colours. For all the projects in this book we have used either the steam-fixed or the iron-fixed varieties. The dyes can be mixed with each other and diluted with water and alcohol, or with a special commercially available diluent. Do not mix dyes from different manufacturers. Try to stay with one brand throughout your project.

When mixing dyes, use white palettes and pots. If you are mixing small amounts, do not pour from the jars: use a dropper instead. When paler shades are required, it is necessary to dilute the dyes using water, alcohol or diluent. You may need to use distilled water rather than tap water, since in some areas tap water contains chemicals and minerals which may affect the colours. When diluting the dye it is best to use a 50% water/50% alcohol mix.

Be sure to check the instructions from the manufacturer on the dye bottle. We recommend that at least 10% of this 50/50 mix is added to the dye, even when a vibrant colour is required. Diluting the dye by this ratio will not change the shade, but will save money and avoid the over-saturation of silk with dye. (Over-saturation can cause problems on washing later on: 'bleeding' sometimes occurs, especially with reds and black, if too much colour has been used; excess dye is rejected on to the fixing paper or runs in the wash.) Obviously paler shades require more of the mixture. Water alone can be used, but we find that the diluent helps smoother applications, especially on large areas.

Iron-fixed dyes differ from the steam-fixed ones in that

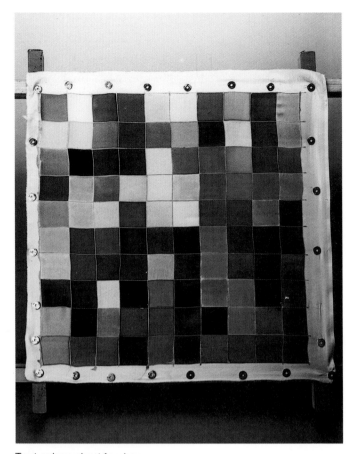

Test colour chart for dyes

there is a white dye available which can be mixed with coloured dyes to create pastel shades. When you have decided on and mixed your colours, we suggest that you draw a test grid with gutta and make a test chart like the one above. You will notice that once the dye has dried out the colour becomes lighter; after fixing it also becomes much more vivid.

When not in use, all dyes should be stored in airtight containers in a cool place. Save diluted and mixed colours in sealed glass or polythene containers for further use.

Fixing

The dye needs to be fixed permanently into the silk to allow it to be washed and to prevent fading. Depending on the dyes used, there are three ways of doing this: steaming, ironing and liquid fixing.

Steam fixing

You can steam your own work at home using a pressure cooker (see picture overleaf). Few people have access to professional steamers, which are expensive and only

viable if you are producing a lot of work. It is, however, worth asking at your silk painting suppliers if they run a steaming service or enquiring at your local dry cleaners, as they usually have a steam box.

The pressure cooker is ideal for smaller amounts of work. Each piece of painted silk must be placed flat on top of several layers of lining paper, craft paper or newsprint without type. Roll the silk and paper together and flatten and seal the ends using strong tape. Tuck the ends towards the centre, then roll and flatten again to form a firm package. The package should be small enough to not touch the sides of the pressure cooker. Fill the bottom of the pressure cooker with about 2 cm (1 in) of water. Place the package in a basket so that the condensation runs down into the water. Seal the lid and cook under pressure for 45 minutes. Turn the heat off, carefully open the lid and remove the package.

After steaming, the colours are more vibrant, and texture of the silk is softer and has a lustrous sheen. If the silk has had inadequate protection in the steamer, water marks or rings may appear on it. Once water marks have been made little can be done to remove them.

Fixing equipment and steamer

Fixing equipment and pressure cooker

Heat fixing

Iron-fixed dyes are fixed by pressing thoroughly with a hot dry iron on the reverse side of the fabric. Set the temperature of the iron as recommended by the dye manufacturer. After heat fixing the silk can be washed and dry cleaned.

Take care when ironing, as coloured and metallic guttas may print on your ironing board; protect with a layer of newsprint without type, or an old pressing cloth.

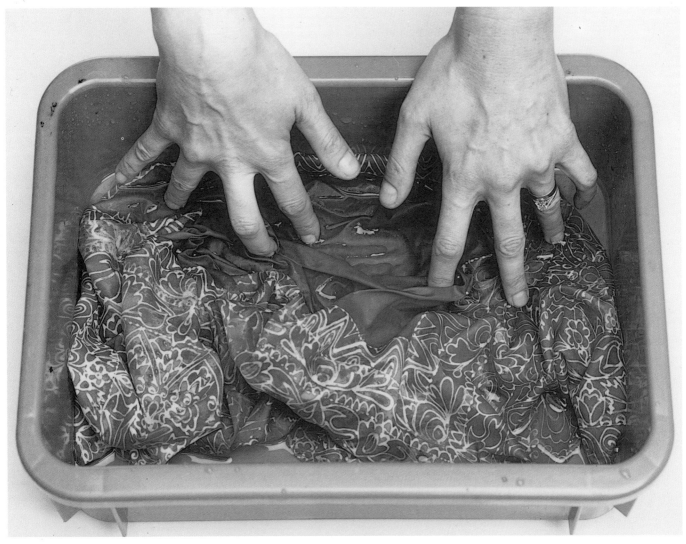

Soaking the silk in liquid fixing solution

Liquid fixing

Liquid-fixed dyes are used in conjunction with silk paint liquid fixer to make them light fast, washable and dry cleanable. Make sure that the silk is dry and then coat on or soak in (depending on the brand) the liquid fixer for approximately one hour. Again, the manufacturer's instructions must be followed, as some fixers need different methods and longer fixing times than others. The silk is then rinsed in cool water to remove excess dye and fixer.

Washing instructions after fixing

After fixing rinse the silk thoroughly in warm water. If water-soluble gutta has been used this will be removed at this stage, leaving a sharp, clear outline. To remove gutta that is not water-soluble, the silk can be dry cleaned or soaked in white spirit. Finally, wash the silk in warm soapy water, rinse and lay on a clean tea towel, roll up and pat to remove the excess moisture. The silk can be ironed while still damp as creases are then easily removed; a fine sheen will appear on the surface of the fabric. If you have used coloured gutta or metallic gutta, do not dry clean the fabric and iron on the reverse side only.

If you have used wax on your silk it will be necessary to wash in white spirit first to remove the last traces. Then wash and iron as normal.

PART TWO

DESIGN and
TECHNIQUES

DESIGN and TECHNIQUES

The designs

Any design can be used when silk painting, but you will soon find that certain designs lend themselves to particular painting techniques. You do not have to be a great artist to try your hand at this craft. Certain techniques, for example the salt technique, require no drawing whatsoever. When using gutta, simple, bold designs work very well. Seascapes and snow scenes are very effective when wax is used, and landscapes lend themselves to the watercolour technique.

Photographs and sketches can be enlarged or reduced in the following way.

Enlarging your design

In this book some of the projects are accompanied by drawings and grids. Enlarge each square to the size indicated and transfer the design to the larger grid. Where drawings are not supplied sketch a design, using our ideas as inspiration or your own. Draw a grid of approximately 2.5 cm (1 in) squares on your original sketch. Decide on the size of your finished work and draw another, larger, grid. This grid must have exactly the same number of squares as are on the original sketch. Working square by square, reproduce the sketch on the larger grid. The same process can be used to reduce the size of a design.

Another way to enlarge or reduce a design is to use a pantograph. These are available at most art and craft shops.

Transferring your design to the silk

Your design must now be transferred to the silk. It is a good idea to make the outline bolder on the paper, using a permanent ink pen, so that the design shows clearly through the silk. Trace the design onto the silk using a soft pencil or a fade-away fabric marking pen (see opposite). The ink disappears after 72 hours – sometimes sooner! – so remember to finish the gutta outline before it vanishes.

To help when tracing, it is best to tape the design and silk to a flat surface to prevent it from moving. The silk is now ready to be stretched on to the frame.

Sometimes clear, simple designs can be seen through a fine silk and it is not necessary to trace the outline. The design can be placed under the frame, close enough to be seen without touching the silk.

Gutta technique

This technique is also known as serti or resist. It involves drawing fine lines of gutta on the silk to outline the design. These lines stop the dyes from spreading into each other. The liquid dyes are then painted directly onto the silk and fixed into the fabric.

Enlarging a design

Faults that may occur when applying gutta

1. The gutta line may appear thick and uneven and start and finish with a big blob. This is because your nib is too large. Replace it with a smaller one.

2. The silk may become smudged or marked with gutta. This may have been caused by a badly-stretched frame, meaning that the silk has touched the work table, or you may have smudged the gutta with your arm or cuff. To prevent these smudges stretch the silk taut; start at the top and work down, or make sure cuffs and loose-fitting clothes do not get in the way.

   To remove unwanted gutta marks, place a folded tissue under the area and rub gently using a cotton bud dipped in the appropriate solvent. This process can be repeated several times to dry and remove the smudge, but sometimes the only way is to cover it and camouflage the mistake by enlarging the design.

3. The gutta may not work properly, causing the dyes to flow over or under the line. The reason for this is that the gutta may have been too thick or too thin. To achieve the correct consistency, see page 12. If the gutta is of a poor quality, there is really no remedy other than to buy another brand. The gutta needs to be more fluid when working on thicker, heavier fabrics.

4. The gutta does not form a continuous line. This may be because of carelessness in the application, meaning that tiny gaps have been left in the gutta line. Check that the line is continuous and go over any opening again before you paint. Be careful not to press too hard or go too fast, as this may cause gaps in the line. Thicker fabrics may need a second application of gutta on the back of the silk.

Tracing the design on to silk

Application of gutta

After deciding on the colour of gutta to be used and the nib size, check the consistency of the gutta. Assemble the pipette, nib and gutta. Holding the pipette like a pen and at an angle of 45 degrees, squeeze steadily and gently so that the gutta flows forming a continuous line (see page 22). Try to pull the pipette towards you, otherwise the top of the pen may catch in the silk. To check that the gutta has penetrated the silk, turn the frame over: you should be able to see a transparent line. It is useful to keep a tissue in your hand as excess gutta sometimes collects around the nib.

Application of dyes

When the gutta is dry you may start painting your design with the dyes (see page 22). For preparing and mixing the dyes see page 14. Paler colours should be applied first, and you will be able to see if you have any 'leaks' of dye seeping over or under your gutta line. Never overload your brush as a little dye goes a long way. The dyes must be worked into the fibres of the silk using the tip of the brush, otherwise uneven colouring may occur. When shading, paint the lighter colours first; then introduce the darker tones while the light ones are still wet. Blend together with the tip of the brush.

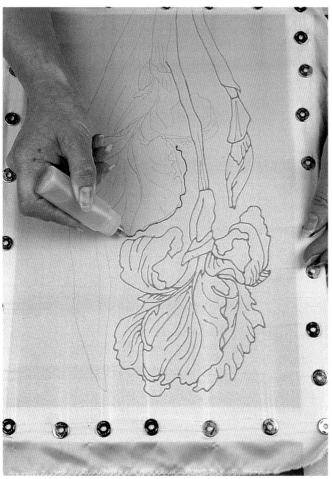

Application of gutta

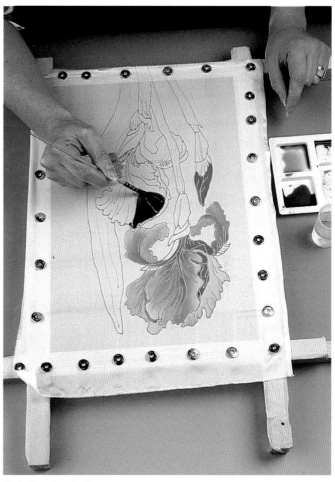

Painting the design

When painting large areas and backgrounds, speed is essential, otherwise water lines or rings will appear on the silk. Large foam brushes or cottonwool can be used. Never re-touch areas that have already dried or paint next to dry paint unless there is a gutta line between the two areas, otherwise a dark line, which is almost impossible to remove, will appear. When you have finished painting and your work is dry, it is ready to be fixed.

Faults that may occur when applying dyes

1. Spots of dye may spill accidentally on either white or an already painted area. Try to remove spots of unwanted dye using cotton buds, tissues and alcohol. Be careful not to use too much alcohol, or the stain will spread. Sometimes this proves unsuccessful. If so, use some creative flair and change your design to incorporate the mistake as a part of the new design. If the cleaning did not work, and on repainting the silk still looks patchy, wet the whole area and sprinkle with salt.

2. The dye may bleed through the gutta line where it is not wanted. This is because of the way the gutta has been

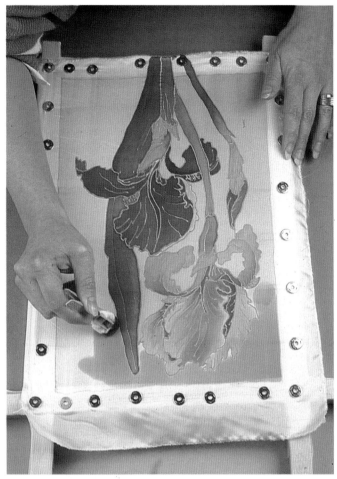

Painting the background

Completed design

applied, although sometimes the dye flows over the lines because the brush is overloaded with dye or through sheer clumsiness. If bleeding occurs quick action is needed. Seal the hole where the dye is escaping with gutta, or sometimes hot air from a hair dryer will stop the flow. Try to remove the dye as in point 1, or improvise.

3. Uneven painting of large areas can result in watermarks. This occurs when the proportions of dye, water and alcohol are incorrect or the dye has been re-applied to areas that have already dried. If the uneven area is a pale colour, it can be repainted using a darker, stronger dye. If this does not work the only solution is to repaint and add texture using salt or alcohol (see pages 26 and 27).

4. Streaks or changes of colour may appear on the silk. This is because the brush or applicator has not been cleaned properly.

5. Marks may be caused by the silk touching the work surface. When painting large pieces of work the wet silk sometimes stretches. To prevent this, keep adjusting the pins to keep the silk taut on the frame.

Wax technique

There is an easy way to get a batik effect without the inconvenience of repeated dipping of the silk in dyebaths as used in the traditional method. This easier method is known as fake or false batik. As with the gutta technique the silk must be stretched taut on a frame. Using molten wax as a resist, apply it to the silk using a brush or a tjanting. Then using a large brush or foam pad, paint the entire surface of the silk. Different colours can be applied to different areas if desired. When the paint is dry, apply more wax to cover the areas you want to remain the first colour and paint again. Keep repeating this process. It is not necessary to remove the fabric from the frame, unless you want a crackled effect, in which case remove the fabric from the frame before applying the final dye colour and crinkle the fabric. Re-pin the fabric and coat with the final dye colour, which will penetrate the cracks to give you the distinctive crackle effect of traditional batik.

Daisies showing the use of wax and cracking

Faults that may occur when applying wax

1. The dye may penetrate the silk under the wax. This is because the wax is not hot enough. Re-wax the reverse side if necessary.

2. The wax may spread too far over the surface of the silk where it is not wanted. This is because the wax is too hot and it has become too fluid. To prevent this, use a test sample to try out the flow of the wax. The only way to remove wax is to soak the silk in white spirit or dry clean, which means that the whole project would need to be re-waxed.

3. Discoloration of the wax may occur if it has not been allowed to harden and cool before the application of the dye. Make sure the wax is cool and hard before applying the dye or unwanted staining may occur.

4. Drips or blobs of wax may have fallen in the wrong place. This often happens, especially when using a tjanting. It is difficult to remove these drips, so keep a tissue underneath to catch them. If mistakes do occur, try to modify the design to include the blobs. Wax must always be ironed off before fixing. Place the silk between clean sheets of brown or absorbent paper and iron until most of the wax has disappeared. A double layer of fixing paper is necessary.

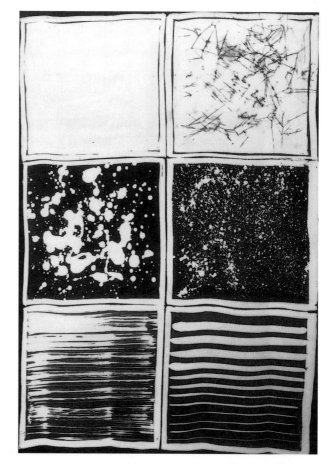

Wax textures, including cracking, dripping, spattering using a brush and tjanting

Using a tjanting

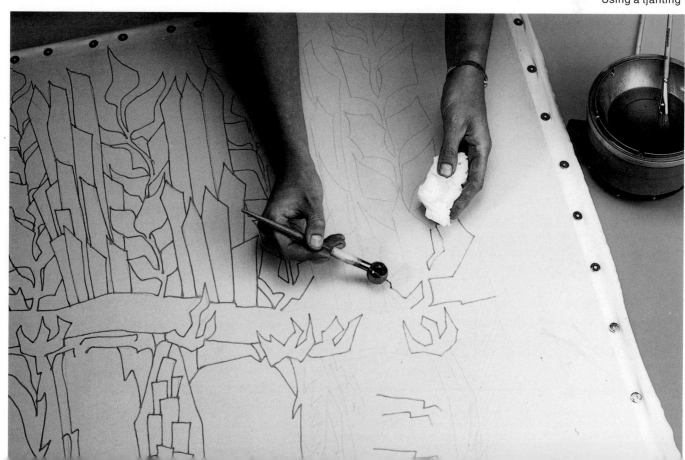

Salt, sugar and alcohol techniques

The effect of salt crystals on dye

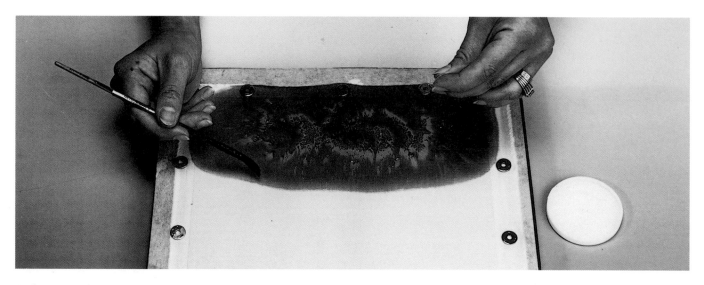

Salt

Place salt on the wet or damp painted colours and allow them to dry. You can see the colours flow as the salt crystals soak up the dye and leave the colour pigments as dark-tones and spots. The salt technique requires the use of water rather than alcohol, which evaporates too quickly and so dries the silk. The end result is always different, depending on the following: the colour and the strength of the dye, the weight and type of silk, the dampness of the fabric and the type of salt used. Even the humidity and room temperature can affect the results. It is difficult to control what happens, but be sure not to use too much salt or to have the silk too wet or the effect will be lost. The salt technique works best with strong, darker dyes or mixed colours. Some colours give far more exciting results than others. It is wise to test them beforehand if the results are vital to a project. Scattering salt at random is effective, especially if several colours are used, as this will produce a mottled effect. You can try to control the results by positioning the salt to produce a specific pattern, for example circles, flowers or bands. The silk should be entirely free from salt before fixing. Once the dyes are dry, brush the salt off.

Silk can be painted with a salt solution to create further effects. Use 250g (9oz) salt to one litre (1¾ pints) of warm water. Dissolve the salt for one hour and then strain the solution through a filter paper. Paint this solution on stretched silk using a Large brush. Leave the silk to dry naturally so the salt texture can form.

Stripes of colour moved using rock salt

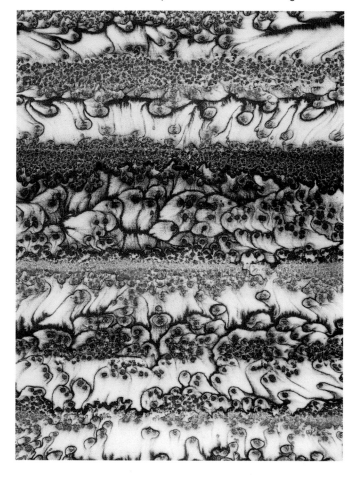

Sugar

This is not quite as exciting as salt, although the sugar crystals do have an effect on the dye if sprinkled on the surface, creating an interesting texture.

The sugar syrup technique can give unusual flowing forms, but be prepared: the drying time of the silk projects can be several days. The sugar solution is made from equal quantities of icing sugar and water. Boil the mixture without stirring until it is reduced by half. The liquid can be used hot or cold. It can be stored in an airtight jar for some time. Re-heat if it goes solid. Drop the thick syrup from a brush or pipette on to the silk. The frame can be horizontal or even upright so that the sugar trickles downwards. Immediately apply the dyes in the gaps beside the syrup. Place the frame flat and leave it to dry. Make sure when fixing that a double piece of paper is used on the silk; this should prevent the concentrated dye from printing through the fixing paper onto the silk during the fixing process.

Effect of sugar syrup on dye

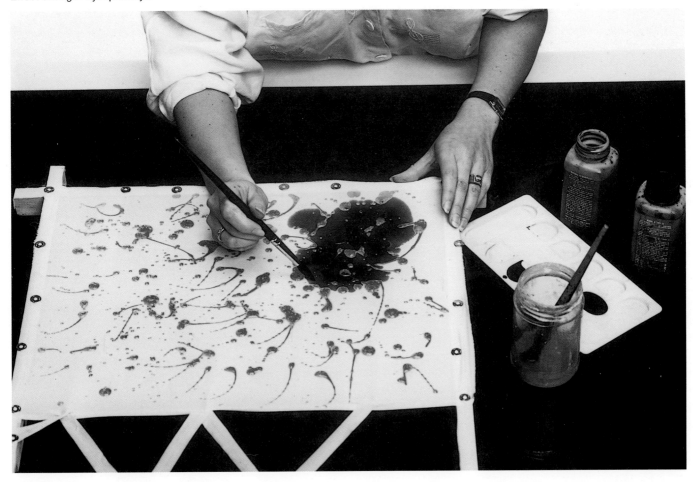

Alcohol

You will find that the stronger the alcohol and dyes, the more effective the results. The textured effect created by the use of alcohol is opposite to the salt technique, as the alcohol disperses the pigment, whereas the salt attracts it (see overleaf). When alcohol is applied to a painted shape or line, the centre becomes paler and the pigment layers itself to the edges. If the process is repeated several times the centre becomes paler and the outside more defined.

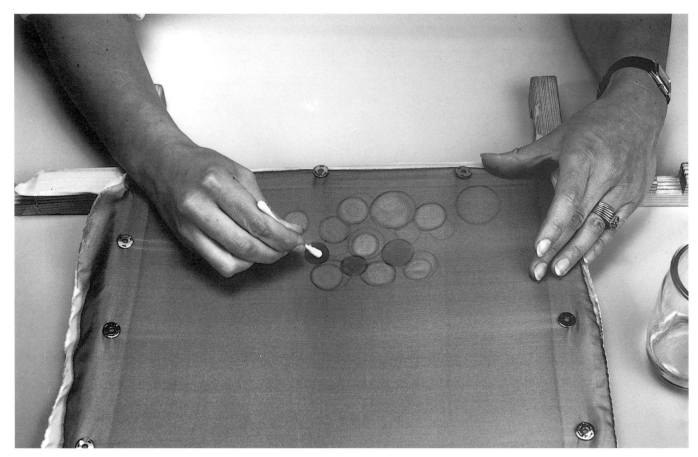

Effect of alcohol on dye

W.atercolour technique

The dyes are unrestrained by the barriers of gutta or wax when using the watercolour technique. First paint the surface of the silk with clear or tinted water, with a diluent, or with a 50/50 alcohol/water solution. Remove excess water with a paper towel. Paint your design while the background is still wet; you will find that the colours move less on a wet background than on a dry one. When two colours are placed close to one another on the fabric, see how they run and blend into each other. The wetter the fabric, the more the colours will run. If you do not want the colours to blend, let the first colour dry before applying the second. A larger line will then form. Try painting with one colour on a wet background, then dipping a second or third colour onto it when wet. The variations to this technique are endless and it is great fun to experiment. Try painting the dyes on dry silk. The dye spreads quickly across the fabric, and by working at speed you can produce some very original work.

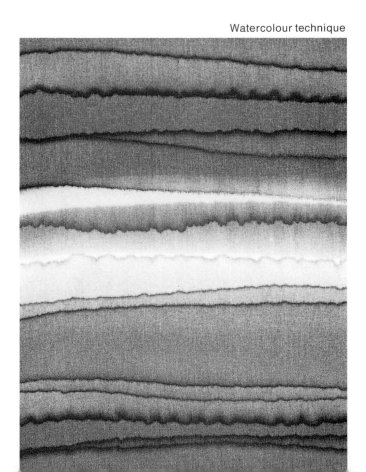

28

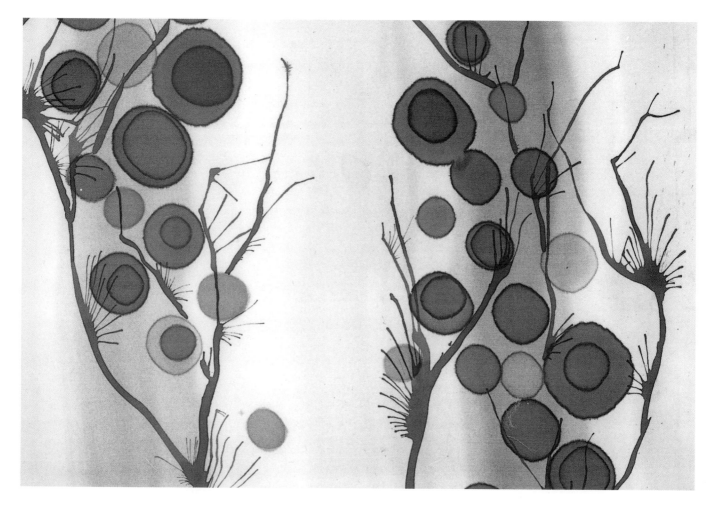

Dye on the surface of the silk after antifusant

Antifusant or anti-spread

Antifusant is also known as stop flow or anti-spread. It is a starch-like fluid used to prevent dyes from penetrating or spreading through the fabric. This allows you to paint directly on to the silk without the dyes spreading. This product is available ready prepared, but it is possible to make your own by mixing solvent and gutta together (we suggest one part of gutta to six parts solvent). The higher the proportion of gutta, the more resistant the silk becomes to the dye.

Coat the silk with anti-spread and allow to dry. Use a cottonwool pad for this; if a brush is used it then has to be cleaned with solvent to remove the gutta. When the anti-spread is dry you can paint directly on to your silk.

Fantastic results can be gained from using this technique with overlaying dyes and combining it with watercolour and salt.

Epaississant or dye thickener

Epaississant, also known as dye thickener, is a colourless glue-like substance. When mixed with the dye this thickener makes it possible to paint directly on the silk without spreading. This is useful when painting fine, detailed work, but its glue-like quality makes it hard to use on large areas when a smooth effect is needed. Alternatively, there is an iron-fix dye on the market which has proved very useful for finer details as it has so thick a consistency. Some of the colours have a slight metallic sheen which is quite attractive.

Stencilling

This technique has always been difficult with steam-fixed dyes, but the new, thicker iron-fix dyes have improved the results tremendously. Some have a metallic sheen which adds to the interest of the colours and enables a greater degree of shading. When the stencil has been prepared on oiled card or acetate, the silk can be stretched out firmly underneath and taped flat to the work surface. Using a flat stencil brush, firmly dab a small amount of dye through the holes. A professional finish can be achieved if more than one colour can be shaded on the same motif. These new dyes do not require the first colour to dry out before others can be added. An interesting combination of techniques is a watercolour or salted background with stencilling on the top.

Christmas design stencil using iron-on dyes

Thick iron-on dyes used for stencilling

Spraying

A spray gun is necessary to achieve even results with this technique, although very interesting textures can be created with a mouth diffuser. Instead of painting a wash background, sprayed colours can give a muted richness to a large area. Quite strong colours can be used, as they lose their strength when sprayed.

A soft effect is achieved by using a spray design on this wisteria

Spraying dye through flower stencil

PART THREE

PROJECTS and
IDEAS

FASHION

SCARVES and SARONGS

Coral reef, hydrangea head and sweet peas. These scarves
illustrate sugar syrup, wax and gutta techniques and the
projects can be found in this section

Never out of fashion, a scarf is an important accessory. Painting on silk is a splendid way to make your own fashion statements. Rolled and twisted at a whim, the scarf is worn more as a fashionable decoration than as a cover-up.

Pure silk, with its infinitely varied weights and textures, can be painted to suit every occasion. Some of the world's most famous artists have been attracted to the magic of a moving canvas. In the 1940's the Hungarian textile designer Zika Asher commissioned work from Henri Matisse, Jean Cocteau and Henry Moore, and the scarves they designed were later displayed in picture frames. You may wish to frame your own scarves, but in this section we hope to inspire you to create wearable art.

The techniques are varied, as are the types of silk used and the sizes of the scarves. The patterns form a guide, but can of course be modified and interchanged to make your own individual creations. Do not be afraid to sign your work: every time a scarf is painted it is an original, because the colours and techniques can never be repeated. The Paris fashion houses of Coco Chanel and Hermes sign their printed scarves, so why not you? Create your own 'Designer' label!

Types of silk

There are many silks that can be used for scarves. The weight and quality must be considered carefully at the beginning of a project, taking into account the finished effect you wish to achieve.

The most effective silk we have found for scarves is pongée no. 9; it is firm but still drapes beautifully without being too expensive.

If luxury is what you are aiming for, then crêpe de Chine is a perfect choice. It is heavier than the pongées and falls into deeper folds. The dyes are enhanced by the twisted yarns which increase the surface texture. Some people find shading more difficult initially with crêpe de Chine, because the dyes need to be worked well into the fabric.

Brocades, too, are luxurious but rather expensive. Often the self-coloured woven pattern can detract from a complicated silk painting on top. Keep the colours and the design simple so that the fabric itself can impress. Scarves needing a lighter, more 'floaty' effect should be made in something like no. 5 or no. 7, or even lovely crêpe georgette or chiffon. These are much more transparent and are ideal for evening stoles or fine summer scarves.

A more traditional look can be gained by using a pongée no. 10, or a twill. The diagonal grain of the twill can be seen on the most exclusive scarves in the shops.

Organza and taffeta are rather stiff silks, but look quite effective as neat neckline scarves or collars, perhaps even edged in fine lace, or beaded.

Silk folded to form a square

Scarf sizes

The size of your scarf depends very much on the finished effect required. The silk is usually cut along the straight grain line which runs parallel to the selvedges. It is easy to make a snip at the selvedge and then the silk can simply be torn across. The tear will be along the grain line.

The normal width of pure silk is 90 cm (36 in). A true square will be the width of the silk. To cut an exact square, fold the corner over to the opposite corner, to form a diagonal. Clip at the point where it touches the selvedge (see picture on page 35).

Here is a list of suggested scarf sizes (in metric):

Large	90 cm × 90 cm
Medium	75 cm × 75 cm
	70 cm × 70 cm
Small	60 cm × 60 cm
Long	45 cm × 150 cm wide
	30 cm × 150 cm narrow (3 per scarf width)

Shawl	120 cm × 150 cm
	90 cm × 90 cm
	120 cm × 120 cm – triangle from 120 cm square
	115 cm × 110 cm – cut on the cross
	115 cm × 150 cm – cut in half lengthways and joined – long
Sarong	90 cm × 150 cm
	120 cm × 150 cm – wide
	120 cm × 200 cm – long and wide

Methods of finishing scarves

Once your silk has been painted and fixed by one of the methods described in Part One, it is ready to be made up into a scarf.

If the gutta is to be removed, the silk should be cleaned at this stage. All scarves should then be washed and ironed (see page 17). Painted pin marks and unwanted edges should be cut away from the silk prior to hemming. Place the silk flat on the work surface. Using a pencil or a fade-away marker pen, rule a line along the

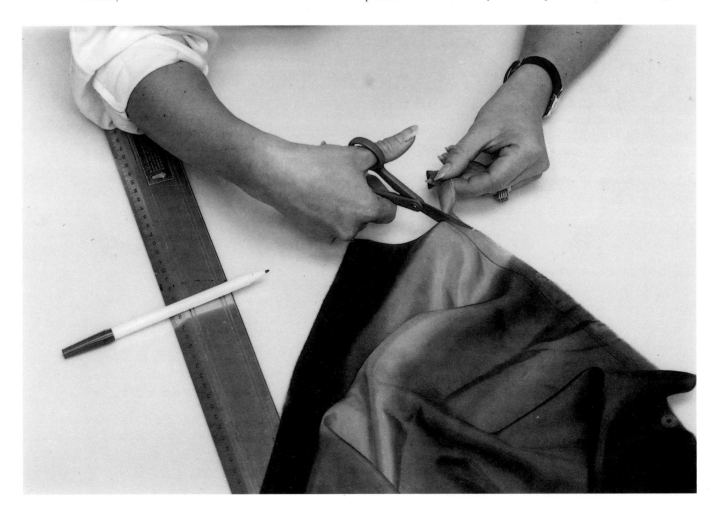

edge of the silk, following the straight grain of the fabric. Remember that at least 1 cm ($\frac{3}{8}$ in) will be taken into the hem if it is hand rolled or machine stitched.

Once it is tidied up, the silk is ready to be hemmed using a fine matching thread. Usually a slightly darker shade of pure silk is recommended, but an ordinary cotton thread could be used instead. Synthetic thread tangles when used for hand sewing and therefore makes the rolling process more difficult.

Silks and sheers require the couture touch of hand-rolled hems. The first thing to catch your eye on any exclusive item is the finish; it takes very little extra effort to impart this same touch and fine workmanship to your own scarves.

Hand-rolled narrow hems

Use this hem to finish your scarves. There are two popular methods, both rather time-consuming and needing practice, but well worth the effort. Never tack this hem or press it heavily afterwards; it should remain fine, soft and rounded.

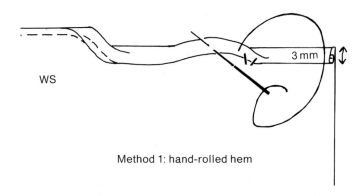

WS

3 mm

Method 1: hand-rolled hem

1.   Machine stitch 6 mm ($\frac{1}{4}$ in) from the raw edge; trim close to the stitching. Roll approximately 3 mm ($\frac{1}{8}$ in) of the edge between the thumb and forefinger, concealing the stitching. Stabilize the roll with the third and fourth finger and slipstitch, taking a single thread with each stitch.

2.   For the second method stitch and trim as above. Turn the edge about 3 mm ($\frac{1}{8}$ in) and crease sharply. Pick up a thread alongside the raw edge. Work in a zigzag pattern, making stitches 6 mm ($\frac{1}{4}$ in) apart. Repeat the process for about 25 m (1 in), then pull up the thread to tighten the stitches and create a roll.

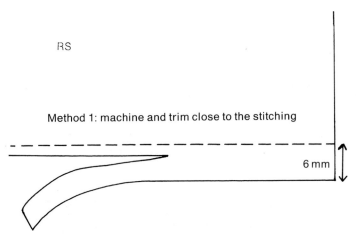

RS

Method 1: machine and trim close to the stitching

6 mm

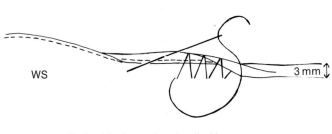

WS

3 mm

Method 2: zigzag hand-rolled hem

For those who cannot face rolling a hem, some, pre-rolled Chinese silk scarves are available.

◄ Cutting off excess silk

Bright yachts sarong

This sarong measures 90 cm × 150 cm (36 cm × 60 in). The surf is painted first of all, using wax, then the yachts are outlined with opaque gutta. A cloudy look is created in the sky by using diluent with pale grey, blue and a touch of pink. The sand is painted using yellow and brown, then salt is sprinkled on to create texture. Finally, the yachts, sea and landscape are painted in.

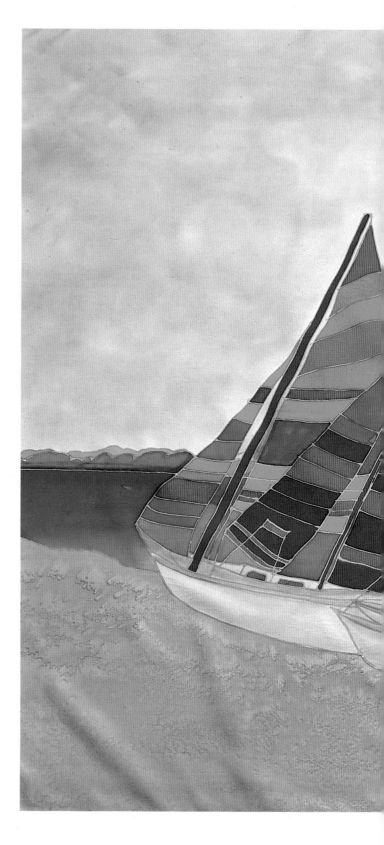

Machine hemming

For those who feel they are unable to hand roll, there are several neat machine methods of rolling a hem.

1. **Narrow straight machine stitched hem.** Turn under 6 mm ($\frac{1}{4}$ in) on raw edge and stitch with a small stitch length close to the fold. Cut away the fabric close to the stitching. Turn under again, encasing the raw edge. Machine stitch the hem in place.

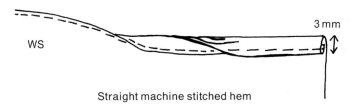

WS   3 mm

Straight machine stitched hem

2. **Narrow zigzag machine stitched hem.** Alternatively, a narrow zigzag machine stitch can give you a fine, quick hem. Turn under on the raw edge 1 cm ($\frac{3}{8}$ in). Press with an iron. Using a fine, close zigzag setting, machine on the

edge of the fold line. Trim off the excess to the edge of the zigzag with sharp pointed scissors.

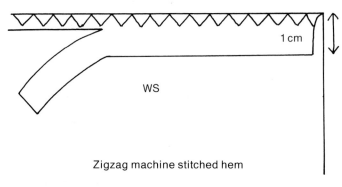

WS   1 cm

Zigzag machine stitched hem

3. **A narrow hemming machine attachment** could be used on the sewing machine to turn a fine straight hem. The foot double folds and machines at the same time. (See the manufacturer's instructions provided with the attachment.) On the fine silk fabric great care must be taken that the corners do not disappear down the throat plate.

Other finishes

Fraying edges. The two vertical sides of a long scarf could be hand rolled leaving the bottom edge to be frayed out for a natural look.

Take a sharp needle or pin and carefully tease out the fibres of silk, leaving the warp threads behind (see picture opposite). It may be difficult to get started, but once the threads are evenly removed there should be no further problems. The fraying could be from 3 cm ($1\frac{1}{2}$ in) or even longer depending on your patience and the desired finished effect.

Double-sided scarves

This is an interesting idea for a long or a square scarf: it could be lined with a co-ordinating or contrasting colour. You might even have a plain side and a patterned side; the scope is endless. Bear in mind that the scarf may not drape so well, as it is thicker, but against that, it will certainly be warmer.

Method

Place the two scarves right sides together.
Tack 1 cm ($\frac{3}{8}$ in) from the edge on all sides.
Machine on this line leaving a 10 cm (4 in) opening in the middle of one side (preferably not a short side on a long scarf).
Remove the tackings and trim off the corners diagonally.
Turn to the right side and slipstitch the opening together invisibly.
Press flat, rolling the seam line right to the edge.

Designing your scarf

This is very personal and depends on many factors, including the purpose for which the scarf is intended, the skill of the painter and also the technique to be used.

Most designs for scarves benefit by having a border. It seems to bring the whole idea together. Sometimes the design can break into a border to cut across the solid line. A much lighter effect is gained when background colour

Fraying out silk fabric

goes to the edges; it seems less formal.

Many times a complicated design is lost because the main design or pattern is placed in the middle of the scarf. Bear in mind that the scarf is usually folded into a triangle so that it is from the centre of the bottom corner. Try drawing your design on tissue paper exactly the same size as your scarf. You can then fold and drape it to see what the effect will be like.

PROJECTS

The following scarf projects are accompanied by brief descriptions of their design and method of painting.

As many of the ideas use the same techniques, we have simply shown photographs in some cases.

Gutta technique	Autumn leaves and fruit
	American patchwork sampler
	Tropical bird
	Sweet peas
	Hot air balloons over
	Connecticut–sarong
Gutta/watercolour	Boatmen's sunset
Gutta/spray	Cellular forms
Wax	Hydrangea heads
	Red poppy
	Lightning
	Ripples
	On the beach
Pastel crayons	Squares and squiggles
Sugar syrup	Coral reef
	Blue lagoon

 GUTTA

AUTUMN LEAVES and FRUIT

Material used: Pongée no. 9
Dimensions: 90 cm × 90 cm (36 in × 36 in)
Technique: Gutta (gold), no. 5 nib

Colours: Bright red, orange, warm brown, dark brown, olive, ivy green

Method

Apply the gutta design (see chart overleaf). Paint one group of leaves at a time and shade using two or three tones of green. Change the shades for another set of colours on contrasting leaf shapes. Do not overload your brush with dye or there will be no opportunity for shading.

The fruit should stand out clearly from the leaves but should also be delicately shaded. Place a deeper tone consistently to one side to round off the shapes.

Remember that the colours of autumn can be quite vivid and varied. The background is painted last in a deep chocolate brown using a large brush or pad of cottonwool.

AMERICAN PATCHWORK SAMPLER

Material used: Pongée no. 9
Dimensions: 90 cm × 90 cm (36 in × 36 in)
Technique: Gutta (gold), no. 5 nib
Colours: Burnt orange, light tan, airforce blue

1 sq = 2 cm

Method

The patchwork design is very complicated as a whole: we have drawn out a combination of squares for you to use (opposite). These can be used systematically or can be drawn on to your silk at random.

The depth of the patchwork design is three full squares with a border of 6 cm (2½ in) at the edges. The thicker gold gutta lines in the centre and on the outside of the design are simply broader scalloped bands of the gold gutta.

The three colours are a combination of burnt orange, light tan and a deep airforce blue. Again, the choice is yours. Alternate the three to make different interesting effects. Here the centre of the design is painted in burnt orange and the outside border in airforce blue.

TROPICAL BIRD

Material used: Crêpe de Chine
Dimensions: 70 cm × 70 cm
Technique: Gutta (gold flower and foliage, navy bird), no. 5 nib; alcohol texture
Colours: Yellow, pale cream, peach, orange warm brown, pale turquoise, leaf green jade, burgundy and navy

1 sq = 3 cm

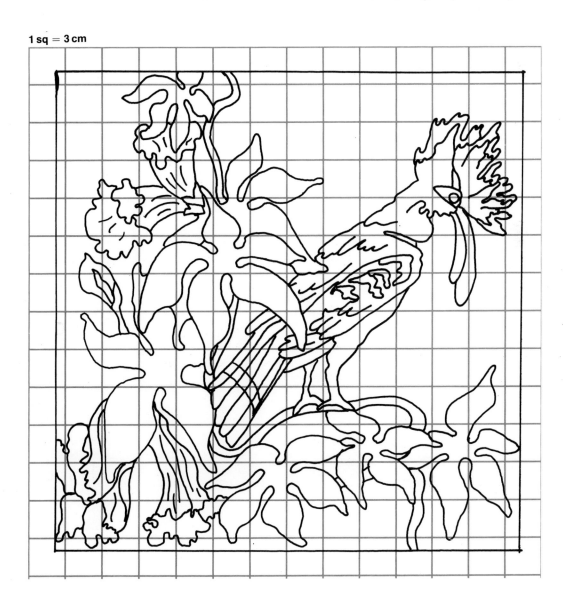

Method

Using the gold gutta first, outline the flowers and foliage. When dry, outline the bird in navy.

Paint the bird in the paler colours first (the yellow and the turquoise/green). Add to it the warmer peach brown tones with a touch of burgundy to enrich the colour. Finally, fill in the dark navy on the wings, tail and head.

The flowers are shades of cream, peach and orange. Do not overload your brush with dye or shading will be difficult; the light edges of the flower tips should be wetted with a little alcohol or water first to stop the dyes from creeping up to the outline.

Use the leaf green with a little yellow for shading on the uppermost leaves. Change to the jade green and add a little navy for the shading on the stems and background leaves.

The centre is a warm peach/brown tone. Dry thoroughly. Then, using the tip of a brush or a cotton bud, dot the surface at the corners with alcohol to create a light texture.

The border is two colours merging, with the navy nearest to the leaves and the burgundy on the outside.

Tropical bird and blue lagoon scarves (see page 63)

SWEET PEAS

See finished design on page 34

Material used: Pongée no. 9
Dimensions: 30 cm × 150 cm (12 in × 60 in)
Technique: Gutta (green on stems, red on flowers, grey on trellis), no. 5 nib
Colours: Pale and deep purple, pale and bright pink, pale and bright red

1 sq = 2 cm

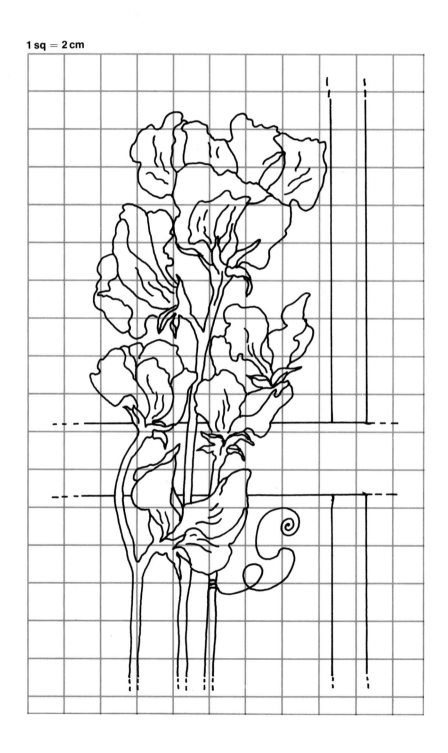

Method

Using the green gutta, outline the stems and sepals. Follow by changing to the red gutta for all the flower heads. The trellis border is in dark grey gutta.

Continue, when dry, to paint the sweet pea flowers. They will need to be painted using a fine brush to achieve the subtle shading. Start with the red on the inner flower, then change to shades of pink, and finally use the purple and minute touches of pink on the outer heads. To help retain some white silk, place dots of either diluent or water on the edges of the individual petals. This painting cannot be hurried if you want to achieve fine, detailed shading.

Paint in the cross stripes in bright pink and deep purple. Tone down these colours with diluent and paint in the background colours pale pink and pale purple.

HOT AIR BALLOONS SARONG

See finished design on pages 50 and 51
Material used: Pongée no. 9
Dimensions: 90 cm × 150 cm (36 in × 60 in)
Technique: Gutta (clear), no. 5 nib
Colours: Pale blue, yellow, red, green, pink, purple, turquoise, light and dark.

Method

Apply gutta as shown below. Dry thoroughly. Paint the sky first using a pale blue dye mixed with diluent. Try to give the idea of distance by lightening the colour near to the skyline. Paint straight over the balloons (the stronger colours will cover these tones).

Using the entire range of bright colours, paint in the balloons as you wish. The people and the baskets are painted in grey and brown. Finally, paint in the hills, again using lighter shades of green in the distance and bottle green in the foreground.

1 sq = 5 cm

Hot air balloons over Connecticut sarong

GUTTA WATERCOLOUR

BOATMEN'S SUNSET

See finished design on page 54

Material used:	Crêpe de Chine
Dimensions:	70 cm × 70 cm (28 in × 28 in)
Technique:	Watercolour, gutta (black) no. 5 nib; sea salt
Colours:	Pale yellow, blue, pale grey, pale orange, blue, burnt orange, dark brown

Method

Using the black gutta, draw over the design and the border lines. Dry thoroughly.

Wet the entire piece of silk with diluent so that the dyes used for the watercolour effect will go on smoothly. Mix the pastel shades of the blue, grey, yellow and orange tones and apply smoothly with a large brush over the background. Keep the sky in predominantly orange and yellow tones to represent the sunset, moving down into the blues and reflected orange by the boats.

You can paint on top of the boats, as these will later be painted over in a darker colour. Never let the background dry as you are working it, as lines will form.

When the watercolour is complete, dry using a hair dryer, then paint in the boats using deeper tones of brown. The sails are stronger tones of burnt orange and brown.

Finally, paint the narrower border burnt orange and the outer border in dark brown. Whilst the dark brown border is damp, sprinkle it with crystals of salt. Wait for these to draw up the dye (usually this process continues until the silk is dry).

1 sq = 4 cm

GUTTA SPRAY

CELLULAR FORMS

See finished design on page 55
Material used: Crêpe de Chine
Dimensions: 90 cm × 90 cm (36 in × 36 in)
Technique: Spray and gutta (colourless), no. 5 nib
Colours: Lemon yellow, pale grey, grey, pale purple, deep purple

Method

Cut out the square of silk and pin loosely into folds on an upright frame. Prepare three shades of dye (lemon yellow, pale grey and pale purple) ready for spraying the background. A spray can was used for this, but an airbrush or even a mouth diffuser would create the same effect. Holding the can at least 25 cm (10 in) away from the silk, start to spray. Try to follow the folds to re-create them with colour. Do not overspray so that the silk becomes wet; several light layers are better than one heavy one. Change your dye to the second colour and try to spray from the underside of the fold this time, rather than on top of the first colour. Unpin the silk and recreate folds and drapes from another side. This will add an extra dimension to your work. Spray with the third colour on these new folds and on the plainer areas.

Carefully remove the folded silk from the frame and stretch it on your frame as normal. Make sure that the silk is dry. Gutta abstract cellular forms on the less interesting areas of the scarf. Using a broad ruler, draw in the border about 6 cm (2¼ in) from the edge. Gutta the border and dry thoroughly.

Paint in the cellular forms using pale and deep purple. Shades of grey can be added to give definition. The border is painted last in a dark grey.

1 sq = 5 cm

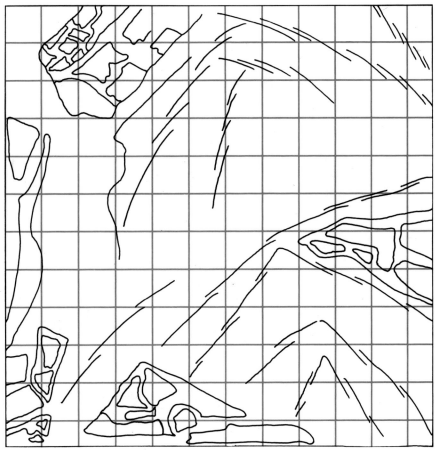

Boatmen's sunset scarf

Cellular forms scarf

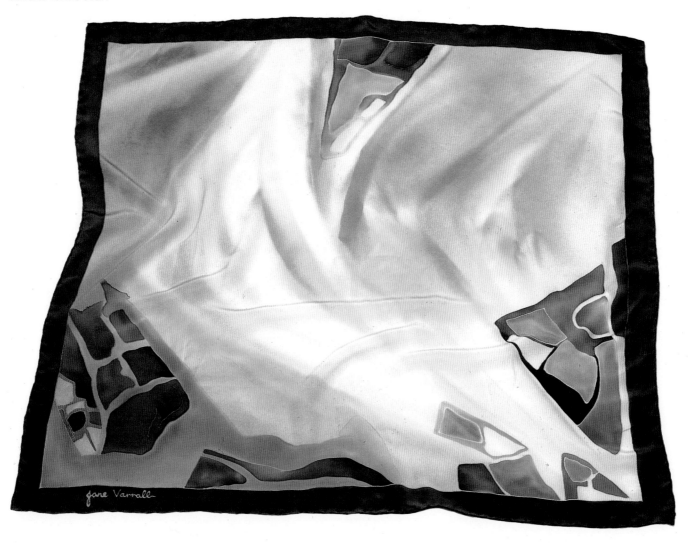

HYDRANGEA HEADS

See finished design on page 34
Material used: Pongée no. 9
Dimensions: 30 cm × 150 cm (12 in × 60 in)
Technique: Watercolour, wax, sea salt
Colours: Pink, pale and deep purple, navy

Method

Position groups of flower heads and leaves randomly on the length of the scarf. Make sure that the leaves and flowers vary in direction. Draw on the silk lightly in pencil. Mix up two shades of pink, a lilac and a pale blue for the wash background colours. Using a large brush, cover the background with random stripes of these colours across the width of the scarf. Heat the wax and paint over half the flower head design, sealing in the first layer of colour. Paint over this with a second wash of stronger pink and blue tones. Dry carefully using a hair dryer, being careful not to melt the wax. Add the final petals to the full hydrangea heads in wax. Also place on the leaves in wax.

Mix up the final purple colour and, using a large brush, cover the entire scarf in an even wash. As the scarf is painted, sprinkle on sea salt crystals. When the silk dries, these will create a random texture. Leave the scarf to dry naturally. When dry, remove the salt and iron off the wax between sheets of absorbent paper. The scarf is now ready for fixing.

1 sq = 2 cm

RED POPPY

See finished design on page 58
Material used: Pongée no. 9
Dimensions: 2 pieces 30 cm × 150 cm (12 in × 60 in)
Technique: Wax
Colours: Red, green, navy blue

Method

Draw the poppy design in the centre of one scarf width. Using a long, straight ruler, draw in the border on each side. Remember to have two poppy heads pointing towards the one in the middle. Heat the wax and, using a medium sized wax brush, cover over the entire background area within the border lines. Paint the green stalks and leaves next, as well as the centre of the flower. Wax over the green, leaving fine gaps around the edges of the leaves. These will be highlighted by the navy blue later on. Paint the red of the poppies and continue the red dye evenly into the borders.

The waxing stage is important. Cover all the red petals individually with wax so there are fine gaps separating them. Paint over the border with wax as well. Remove the whole scarf from the frame and lightly crack all over the centre; it is through these cracks that the navy dye will permeate, giving the 'batik' effect. Paint navy blue over the scarf centre taking care not to put dye on the border, as it will spoil the crisp, clean effect. If this occurs, clean it off immediately with cottonwool.

Remove the wax when the silk is dry. It is now ready for fixing. Paint the remaining length of silk in the same red as the poppies, using a pad of cotton wool or a large brush. This is a double-sided scarf (see page 40).

1 sq = 2 cm

LIGHTNING

See finished design on page 59
Material used: Crêpe Georgette
Dimensions: Triangle cut from 120 cm × 120 cm
  (48 in × 48 in) square. It is easier to pin
  the whole square to a frame and draw
  in the diagonal with gutta.
Technique: Wax, salt and watercolour
Colours: Lilac, pale bright blue, strong bright
  blue, shocking pink, cherry red, yellow

Method

Heat the wax and draw on the wax lightning forms using a tjanting. Thicken the central column, drawing more finely towards the edges.

Wet the crêpe with diluent all over; start to paint with the cherry red and shocking pink near to the wax lines. Add bright yellow streaks, then fade into the purple tones. At this stage you may want to sprinkle on some sea salt to start the reaction with the purple, but take care that you do not dislodge it when continuing to paint the surrounding blue. Add extra tones of blues and pinks towards the edges. Leave to dry naturally and remove the wax. The scarf is now ready for fixing.

Red poppy double-sided scarf (right). Gutta technique is used
on the scarf on the left which shows a colourful rose design.

Lightning and ripples scarves

On the beach sarong

RIPPLES

See finished design on page 59
Material used: Crêpe georgette
Dimensions: Triangle cut from 120 cm × 120 cm
                      square (48 in × 48 in)
Technique: Wax
Colours: Tan brown, pale blue/grey, navy blue
                      with a hint of purple

Method

Paint the whole scarf with a wash of two colours (the grey blue and the tan brown). They can be applied in rough, rounded shapes of colour. Take care not to leave any white areas unpainted. Dry with a hair dryer.

Using a fan-shaped wax brush, wiggle light lines of wax over the whole area of the scarf. Some can cross over at right angles. With a large brush or cotton wool pad, cover the entire scarf with navy blue. Leave to dry naturally. Remove the wax. The scarf is now ready for fixing.

ON THE BEACH – SARONG

See finished design on page 59
Material used: Pongée no. 9
Dimensions: 90 cm × 150 cm (36 in × 60 in)
Technique: Watercolour, wax, sea salt
Colours: Turquoise, navy, royal blue, jade,
                      yellow, light tan, brown

Method

Wax in the white parts of the sunshades and the deck chairs using a medium-sized wax brush. At this stage you also need to wax in the waves at the shoreline. They need to form a continuous barrier for the blue dye, but should not look too solid; try flicking the brush tip with your fingertip to spray the wax upwards on to the sea area.

Mix a pale turquoise blue shade with diluent and paint across the top of the silk to a depth of about 20 cm (8 in); try to vary the tone to indicate clouds. Dry carefully with a hair dryer. Do not melt the wax.

Apply a broad band of wax across the skyline on top of but at the base of the sky colour. Then paint the darker blues of the sea below this line, up to the waves. (**Note**: There should be no white line between these two sections.)

Paint in the jade, blue and turquoise of the sunshades. Wipe off any colour which falls on the white wax.

Finally, paint in the sand using the bright yellow and light tan. Vary the shading over the beach; sprinkle salt on while wet for extra texture. Iron off the wax and fix between two sheets of paper.

PASTEL CRAYONS

SQUARES and SQUIGGLES

See opposite and finished design on page 62
Material used: Crêpe de Chine
Dimensions: 90 cm × 90 cm (36 in × 36 in)
Technique: Dye pastel crayons, steam fix, dyes
Colours: Crayons: beige, turquoise, purple,
                      mauve, black
                      Dyes: tan, pink, purple, olive, navy
                      blue

Method

Stretch the silk out on a frame. Using a dye pastel crayon, firmly draw the framework of the design using the chart opposite. Change colours frequently and add the shapes and symbols within the squares. The crayons must be applied strongly, or they will not form a resist for the dyes. Melt the lines with a hair dryer. Paint in your dye colours randomly. Try to space them out evenly. Do not paint the dyes on too heavily, or they will creep under the barrier created by the crayons. Also, for the same reason, try to paint beside a squiggle or motif rather than over it. Remove the silk when dry. Remember when fixing to add extra paper to absorb the wax.

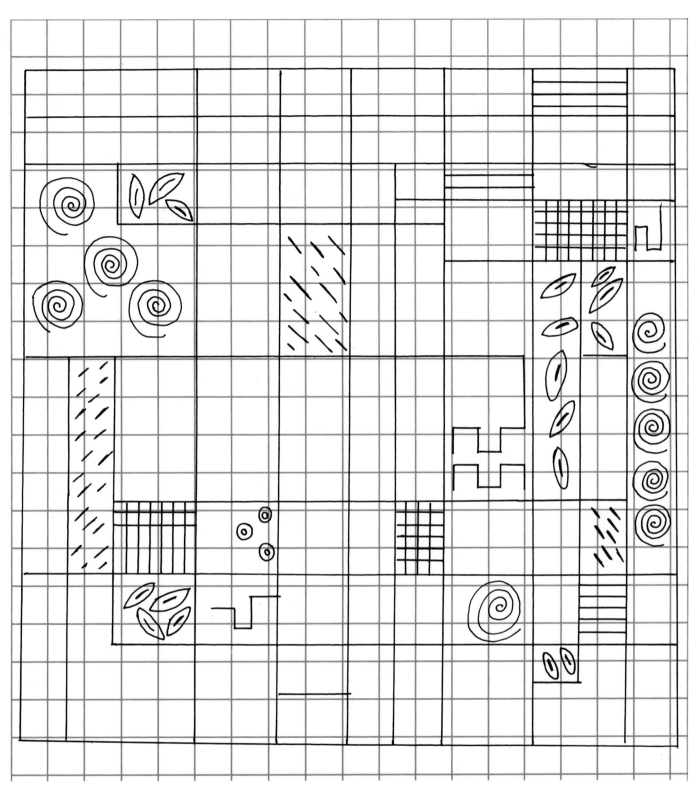

Squares and squiggles

1 sq = 5 cm

Squares and squiggles scarf

$\mathcal{S}$UGAR $\mathcal{S}$YRUP

CORAL REEF

See finished design on page 34
Material used: Crêpe de Chine
Dimensions: 2 pieces 30 cm × 150 cm (12 in × 60 in)
Technique: Sugar, syrup, watercolour
Colours: Tan brown, red, pink/burgandy, grey

Method
Warm up the sugar syrup (use the recipe on page 27). Stretch the two pieces of silk 60 × 150 cm (24 in × 60 in) as a whole on the frame. Draw a pencil line down the centre for the back and front. Stand the frame upright on the floor resting against a wall. Using a large brush, not necessarily an expensive silk painting brush, drip the sugar syrup down one half of the silk. Make sure you have placed newspaper underneath the frame as this technique is rather messy! The idea is to create long streaks at random and of varying lengths and thicknesses.

Pour your colours into jam jars and then drip these down the silk on top and beside the sugar streaks. Make the silk quite wet with the dyes so as to create a reaction with the sugar. Leave the frame upright for several hours. Keep the colours used on the front half of the scarf; they can be used for the second half which will be shaded using the watercolour technique.

Lay the frame back on a table and, using a large brush, paint soft stripes of all the colours along the length of the second side. Try to blend the colours smoothly where they join. Pale colours should always be mixed with diluent for smooth shading. (See information on watercolour techniques on page 28.)

Allow the sugar syrup to dry; this may take up to three days. The silk can then be fixed, using a double piece of paper, separately from the other work.

BLUE LAGOON

See detail below and finished design on page 47
Material used: Crêpe de Chine
Dimensions: 115 cm × 90 cm (46 in × 36 in)
Technique: Sugar syrup
Colours: Emerald, turquoise, ivy green, purple/blue, navy blue

Method

Warm up the sugar syrup (use the recipe on page 27). Stretch the silk on a frame. Keep the frame flat on the table. Drip the sugar syrup on the silk, using an old brush; put plenty on in blobs of different sizes. Paint around the sugar with all the colours. Make the silk quite wet with the dyes, so that the whole piece is painted.

Continue to drip more sugar syrup on top of the wet dyes; they will continue to react for some time. Leave for two or three days until the syrup has dried. Fix separately from other work. Use at least double thickness of paper.

Blue lagoon scarf – detail

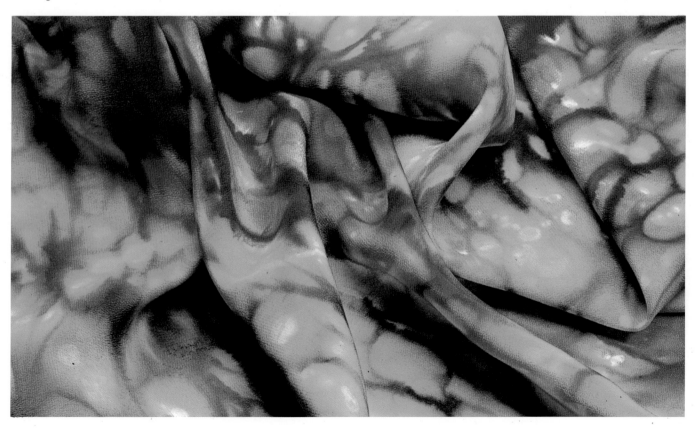

Silk fabric feels wonderful next to the skin and is ideal for special tops, either for day wear or for the evening. We have chosen some very simple styles which can be sewn easily by the average dressmaker.

Patterns

The pattern layouts are intended as a guide for your silk painting rather than as an accurate cutting layout. They will help you decide on placing of colours, textures and motifs on the fabric. Remember that all the painting is done on square or rectangular pieces of silk with the pattern shapes drawn on. These are then cut out accurately to size after the fabric has been fixed.

Try to choose a very basic pattern for your first attempts. Avoid darts, pleats and tucks. Often, the simpler the pattern, the more effective your silk painting will be. Silk drapes so well and has such a natural sheen that it will not be necessary to incorporate elaborate sewing techniques.

Commercial patterns are available in styles similar to those we describe here. Simply cut out the pattern shapes and lay them on your silk fabric as shown on the commercial pattern layout. Draw on your pencil and gutta outline at least 2 cm ($\frac{3}{4}$ in) larger than your pattern so that the seam allowances will be painted in coloured dye. Nothing looks worse than white background creeping into your garment or pin marks from the silk painting.

Design

Keep your designs simple. Colours can be vibrant for stunning impact – see the camisole top and bag on page 66 – or subtle for tasteful classical styles, as shown in the jackets. The designs can be minimal, to show one or two painting techniques to great effect: gutta, watercolour, salt, antifusant and wax have all been used in this section. The placing of a motif is important: make sure it is not too low on a blouse so that most of it is tucked away into skirts or trousers. On a top, remember that the seam allowances encroach into a neckline shaping, so do not place a motif too near an edge. The eye can also be drawn away from areas which you may not want to accentuate – for example, place a bird or flower motif on the shoulder and neckline rather than on the bustline if you have a heavy bosom. Remember the back of your garment. The design could continue over the shoulder on to the back, or a small part of the larger front design could be placed on the back for eye-catching detail.

Draw the design on to the actual pattern piece to ensure the correct positioning; the proportion of the design is important.

Type of silk

We have used crêpe de Chine as the main fabric in most of these examples, as it is slightly thicker than the pongée and therefore not so 'see through' when painted in pale shades. It also hangs and drapes beautifully because of its extra weight.

Pongée no. 9 was used for several of the simpler tops and also for the lining of the jackets. A heavier pongée could also be used for any of the tops. Other silk types could include satin brocade, twill and soie sauvage. The latter does not drape softly, but is ideal for jackets and skirts.

Any materials that you use with the silk should be dry cleanable or washable. Pre-shrink cottons if they are to be used as lining fabrics.

Sewing silk on the machine

Many people are afraid to use a fine fabric such as silk, claiming that it is too difficult to sew. This is not the case if a few points are considered beforehand.

- Always cut out the fabric using very sharp scissors to avoid snags.

- Carefully pin and tack the seams so that they do not move under the presser foot.

- Choose a suitable seam for the garment. Flat seams with small zigzag finish or french seams are recommended. We prefer to see the neat finish of a french seam on tops which are unlined (see diagrams opposite).

- Make sure that your needle is fine and has a sharp point. Renew regularly if snags occur.

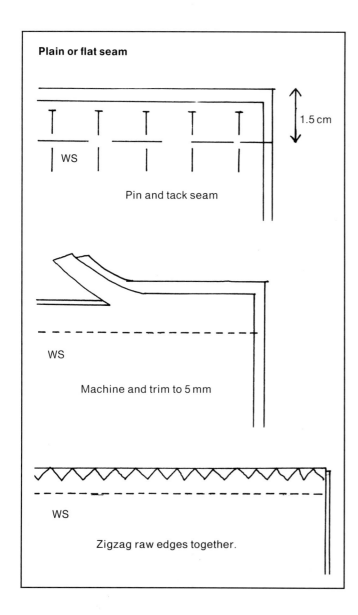

Plain or flat seam

1.5 cm

WS

Pin and tack seam

WS

Machine and trim to 5 mm

WS

Zigzag raw edges together.

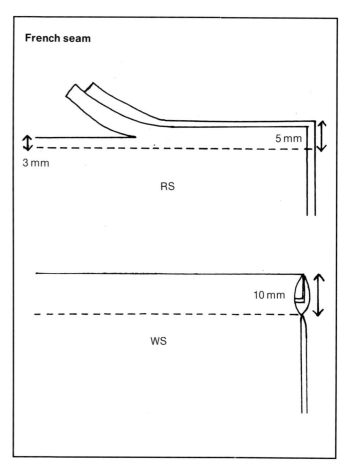

French seam

3 mm

5 mm

RS

10 mm

WS

● Use a small stitch length and stretch the silk slightly as you feed it under the presser foot. This will allow a little extra 'give' so that the seam line does not look too tight.

● Sewing thread should preferably be of pure silk although, if this is not available, a good quality cotton and synthetic mixture could be used instead.

● Always use a steam iron and press regularly throughout the construction of the garment.

● Hems and necklines on blouses can be machined using a narrow, fine straight stitch edge or by hand rolling the edge (see page 37). Those of you with machines which have the facility of special embroidery patterns could simply sew a decorative finish on the neckline or hems for a pretty and unusual edging.

PROJECTS

BUTTERFLY CAMISOLE

See finished design on page 66
Finished size: Dress size 10–12 (38–40)
Material used: Crêpe de Chine
Fabric requirement: 45 cm × 92 cm (18 in × 37 in) – bodice
15 cm × 92 cm (6 in × 37 in) – straps straps and butterfly
30 cm × 90 cm (12 in × 37 in) – wadding
70 cm × 92 cm (28 in × 36 in) – bag
Technique: Salt – bodice, straps and bag
Antifusant – butterflies
Appliqué – butterflies
Colours: Fuchsia, pink, bright purple

Method

Paint the whole piece of bodice silk, strap and bag in shades of purple and fuchsia pink. Salt the wet surface to create textures. Allow to dry. Coat a small square of silk, 10 cm × 10 cm (4 in × 4 in) with antifusant and delicately paint on butterfly shapes. Paint three or four so that the better two can be chosen. Fix as normal. For methods of appliqué, see opposite.

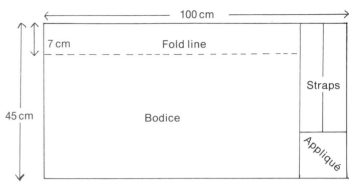

Pattern layout of camisole top

Sewing up the garment

1. Cut out the bodice and strap pieces.

2. Machine along foldline as shown in diagram.

3. Press to form a fold.

4. Tack centre back seam. Adjust the size at this stage.

5. Machine back seam (see diagram on french seam, page 65)

6. Machine length of the straps, wrong side facing. Turn to right side. Tuck under ends. Hem. Adjust to fit.

7. Sew on to bodice at front and back. Machine under fold line. Hand sew invisibly at the top edge.

8. Machine narrow hem on bottom edge of camisole.

9. Sew on detached appliqué butterflies.

Camisole top and matching piped clutch bag. Separate painted butterflies are applied to the shoulder

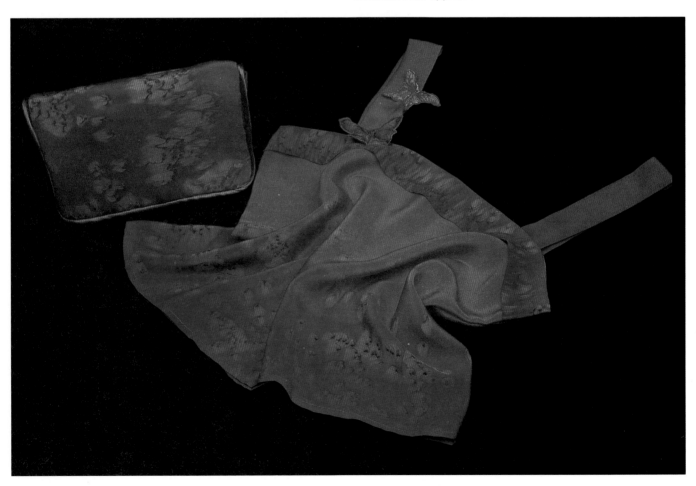

Appliqué

This is a separate piece of fabric which is sewn to a larger piece of fabric as an extra decorative motif. There are two ways in which you could make your appliqué and apply it to the background fabric:

Detached appliqué

1. Paint the silk motif, fix, wash and iron flat.

2. Sandwich three layers of material together – the painted top piece, the wadding in the centre and the silk or backing fabric underneath. Using a pointed needle and working from the middle, baste (large tacking) the layers together. Keep all the layers smooth. This stage of preparation is very important to the final finish of the piece.

Preparing and sewing butterflies for appliqué

Effective gutta graffiti in gold and black enhances these three tops (see Method on page 70)

3. Using the zigzag setting, machine a satin stitch around the motif. The stitch length is nearly 0 and the stitch width approximately 2 mm ($\frac{1}{16}$ in).

4. Clip off the ends of the machining and trim excess silk very close to the machine stitches, using small sharp pointed scissors.

5. Small pieces of appliqué finished in this way will tend to 'curl'; either lightly steam flat or leave to give a three-dimensional effect, as with the butterfly.

6. Sew by hand on to the garment. Appliqué could be easily removed if sewn to garments which cannot be washed. The silk is washable.

Appliqué trapunto

1. Roughly cut out your shapes to be appliquéd.

2. Tack to the background fabric in final position.

3. Using small satin stitch, zigzag around the motif. Trim to stitches using sharp, pointed scissors.

4. Turn to the inside of the garment and make a small slit in the centre of the shape following the grain. Gently push in padding from behind with a knitting needle. Fill until the surface is sufficiently raised.

5. Close the slit by oversewing the edges neatly together.

6. The shell design below was then quilted along the centres in running stitch to create extra texture.

GREEN and BLUE STRIPED TOP

Finished size: Dress size 10–12 (38–40)
Material used: Crêpe de Chine
Technique: Watercolour
Colours: Jade green, dark blue

Method

Paint the whole silk green. When dry, apply one layer of pale blue stripes down the length of the silk. Dry with a hair dryer. Using slightly stronger blue dye, paint on some more stripes to create fluted edges. Dry with a hair dryer. Fix as normal.

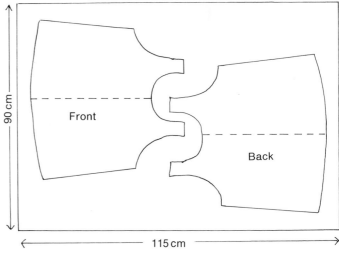

Pattern layout for green and blue top

Sewing up the garment

1.   Cut out as in the diagram.

2.   Machine shoulder and side seams using french seam (see page 65).

3.   Roll neck and armhole edges. Roll up the hem (see page 40).

4.   Press lightly.

'LADY'S LACE' TOP

Finished size: Dress size 12–16 (40–42)
Material used: Crêpe de Chine
Technique: Gutta (clear), watercolour
Colours: Pale yellow, peach, green

Method

Using a wide nib, no. 7, draw on the 'lace' effect for the front design in clear gutta. Allow to dry. Paint the three colours in broad bands across the silk, allowing the dyes to dry between the application of each colour so that some interesting edges are created. Fix as normal.

Sewing up the garment

Follow the instructions given for the striped top opposite.

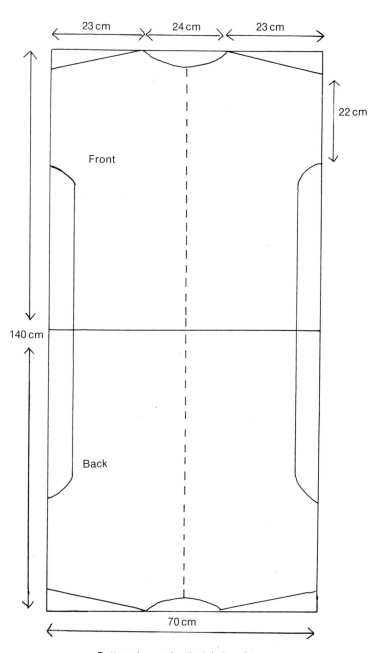

Pattern layout for 'lady's lace' top

RED WHITE and BLACK GRAFFITI TOPS

See finished designs on page 67

These three tops are included to show the effect of simple gutta designs on silk. The silks themselves were not hand painted, but bought and used in their original colours.

Very dramatic designs can be created using gutta:

1. The red top has a black gutta 'squiggle' repeated all over the surface both front and back.

2. The white top uses black and gold gutta alternately, forming a triangular design both back and front.

3. The black silk top looks exceptionally good with a large gold gutta design repeated all over the front and back of the silk. Great care should be taken when ironing – always use a steam iron on the wrong side of the fabric. Do not dry clean gold or coloured gutta, as the particles will be removed.

Sewing up the garments

Follow the cutting layout for 'lady's lace' top on page 69 and sewing instructions for the top on page 68.

Quilted daffodil top

QUILTED DAFFODIL TOP

Finished size: Dress size 10–12 (38–40)
Fabric requirement: 90 cm × 90 cm (36 in × 36 in) crêpe and pongée
Material used: Crêpe de Chine (outside), pongée no. 9 (lining)
Domette for quilting
Technique: Wax, quilting
Colours: Cream, yellow, green, purple, navy

Method

Using a few daffodils as inspiration, roughly draw their shapes on the front square of crêpe de Chine. Paint in pale cream and purples for the outer petals. Dry, then wax over the cream in petal forms. Add dye in bright yellow to the centres of the flower trumpets. Paint some purple and green in the very middle. Allow dyes to merge and flute out at the edges. Paint leaves in cream and green. Dry, then cover all areas to be kept in wax. Paint over the background in dark navy with flashes of green and purple. Paint the back of the top in navy, green and purple as for the front. Paint lining for the top in navy.

Sewing up the garment

1. Follow the cutting layout for 'lady's lace' top on page 69. Baste together the front and back sections in their three layers: the painted silk on top, the domette wadding, and the pongée lining as the backing. Do not cut out the pattern pieces at this stage as the quilting will shrink the fabric.

2. Lightly quilt the front of the top on the flower petals and in some of the centres using a running stitch.

Method of quilting

There are several stitches which can be used for quilting:
straight machine stitch
machine zigzag stitch
hand back stitch
running stitch
reverse chain stitch

The choice of stitch depends on the finished effect required. In many cases the simple running stitch is the most useful, as it is quick and easy to sew. It also makes a less definite outline which does not detract from the silk painting but just adds to the decorative texture.

The type of wadding used depends again on the final effect required. Usually the garment needs to remain soft and supple, so a domette would be preferable. Terylene wadding can also be used, although it is much thicker.

3. Cut out the back and front. Machine together across the shoulders and down the sides.

4. Neaten inside seams by making a flat fell seam.

5. Turn under the hem, armholes and neckline and sew neatly to the lining.

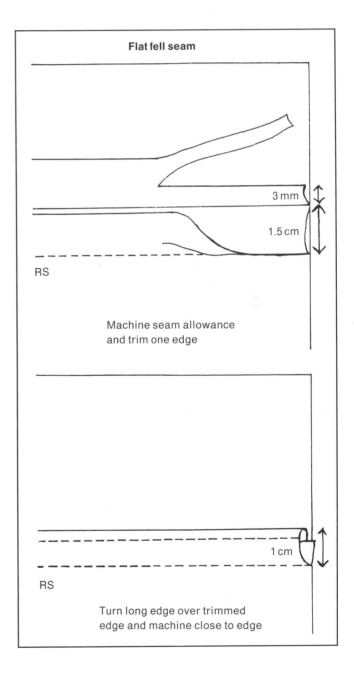

Flat fell seam

3 mm

1.5 cm

RS

Machine seam allowance and trim one edge

1 cm

RS

Turn long edge over trimmed edge and machine close to edge

KIMONO and JACKETS

These three stunning garments show the full potential of silk painting and using the fabric to make original pieces of work. We recommend that you buy commercial patterns of similar designs to create these unique garments accurately, although we do give approximate fabric requirements in all three projects. Draw your designs in the pattern pieces and trace them in the correct position on your silk.

WATER LILY KIMONO

See finished design on page 74

Material used:	Crêpe de Chine, pongée no. 9 lining
Fabric requirement:	Approximately 4 m × 90 cm (4½ yd × 36 in) each
Technique:	Gutta (gold), no. 6 nib
Colours:	Vivid greens, cream and yellow. Navy background

SHORT ART NOUVEAU JACKET

Method

Draw the waterlily design on the back and two fronts of the kimono. You will need a 1.5 m (1¾ yd) length frame to do this. Gutta the outline in gold and paint in the subtle shades of the cream and yellow waterlilies. Paint in the bright apple green and emerald of the waterlily pads; shade to create interest. Paint the whole of the background navy. Paint a piece of silk bright green to edge the arms and bind the neckline. The waist ties could be in either green or navy.

Material used:	Crêpe de Chine, pongée no. 9 lining
Fabric requirement:	Approximately 2.5 m (3 yds) each
Technique:	Gutta (black), watercolour
Colours:	Pinks, red, grey blue

Method

Paint as for jacket opposite, but when the background is dry lightly paint some abstract lines in blue.

THREE-QUARTER LENGTH ART NOUVEAU JACKET

See finished design on page 75

Material used: Crêpe de Chine (jacket), pongée no. 9 (lining)

Fabric requirement: Approximately 3 m (3½ yd) each

Technique: Gutta (black)

Colours: Avocado green, pinks, lilacs and navy blue

Diagram: Design taken from an original Brussels fresco

Method

Draw the stylized lady in her flowing gown on the left front of your pattern. The flowers were placed at random on the sleeves, front and back of the garment. The lady was painted in subtle shades of pinks and lilacs with the deeper pinks on the formal roses. The base and leaves are in navy and green. The background was painted using a pale avocado green. The contrasting lining is pink with a hint of grey.

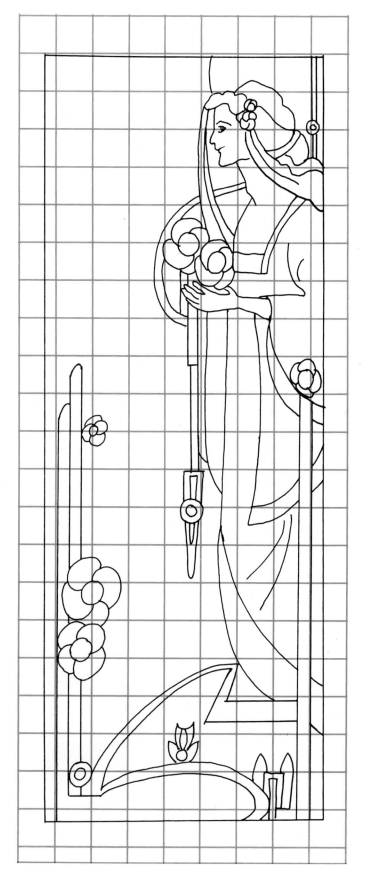

1 sq = 4 cm

73

A bold waterlily design is applied in gold gutta onto this full-length kimono

Art Nouveau three-quarter length jacket in Crêpe de Chine, lined with contrasting pink pongée

Waistcoats have seen a fashion revival over the past few years. The three models here are each in a different style using a variety of silk painting techniques.

Your waistcoat will certainly be an original and can be specially made to link with other items in your wardrobe to create a co-ordinated designer touch. It can be worn either in the daytime or for a special evening occasion.

It is not necessary to paint the whole waistcoat yourself. Maybe you could paint the front and buy a matching or contrasting lining for the back and inside. We have painted the whole garment to make it that little bit special.

You may want to buy a commercial pattern to make up your waistcoat, as they vary in cut from season to season. Try to find a pattern that does not break into the front pieces with darts or bust shaping, as this may spoil your design when it is sewn up. If it is not possible to do this, try to take into account where the darts will come and calculate the design around it, or paint an all over pattern that will not show up the shaping so much.

A simple motif carefully placed on a front can look interesting. Complicated designs are often just not necessary.

QUILTED GRAPES WAISTCOAT

See finished design on page 78
Finished size: To fit size 10–12 (38–40) approximately
Material used: 90 cm × 80 cm (36 in × 32 in) soie sauvage, back and front
90 cm × 80 cm (36 in × 32 in) crêpe de Chine, back and front lining
50 cm (20 in) wadding for quilted areas
Matching thread
Synthetic lining behind quilting
Technique: Gutta (black), salt
Colours: Deep purple, pale greens and pinks, amber

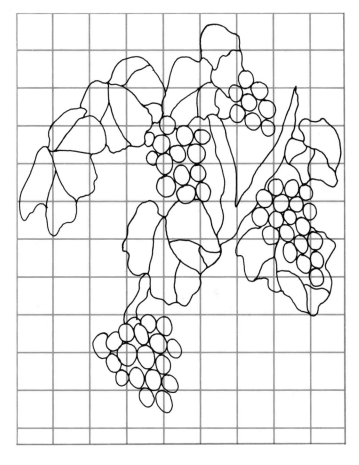

1 sq = 2 cm

Method

1.   Mark out the pattern pieces with a good margin for seam allowances and allowing extra for shrinkage with the quilting. Draw the design on to the soie sauvage.

2.   Stretch the silk, and gutta the leaves and grape design. Use a large nib (no. 7 or no. 8) so that the gutta will penetrate through the thick silk. Check the back and re-gutta if necessary.

3.   Paint in the leaves and branch in greens and pink tones and shade the grapes carefully in pinks and purples. Dry thoroughly.

4.   Mix up a large quantity of pink and amber dyes. Using a large brush, paint evenly across the background, starting with the pink and gradually changing to the amber for the main body of the waistcoat. A touch of purple may be added at the points. Sprinkle sea salt lightly on the waistcoat, from the middle to the base, to add texture and a rich colour variation. Leave to dry. Paint the crêpe de Chine lining a plain deep purple.

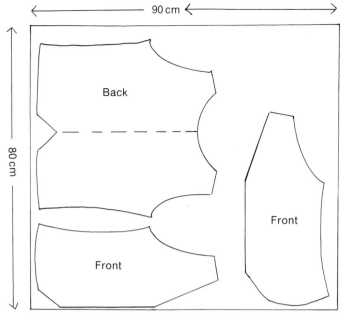

Quilted waistcoat pattern

Close-up of waistcoat back

Sewing up the garment

1.   Cut out the soie sauvage allowing 2 cm ($\frac{3}{4}$ in) extra for quilting. Cut out the lining according to the pattern to make it slightly smaller.

2.   Quilt some of the leaves and grapes to give an extra dimension to your work (see quilting on page 71).

3.   Adjust the front and back size of the waistcoat after quilting. Pin, tack and stitch the fronts to the back at shoulder seams. Do the same to the lining.

4.   Matching shoulder seams, right sides together, pin, tack and stitch the lining to the waistcoat at the armhole, neck, front and lower edges. Clip the seams well at the curves.

5.   Turn the waistcoat to the right side, pulling the garment through the shoulder and out through the side seam.

6.   Press. Pin, tack and stitch the front and back of the waistcoat together at the side seams.

7.   Press under seam allowances on the lining and neatly oversew together to finish off the seams.

8.   Give a final press to the waistcoat.

Different styles of waistcoat using wax and gutta techniques: quilted grapes waistcoat, waistcoat A (left), waistcoat B (right)

WAXED WAISTCOATS A and B

The two waistcoats, right and left, have different patterns, but use the same wax techique.

Finished size: To fit size 10–12 (38–40)
Material used: 65 cm × 90 cm (26 in × 36 in) soie sauvage, fronts and belt
150 cm × 90 cm (60 in × 36 in) pongée no. 9, back and lining
Extras: 4 buttons
Technique: Wax
Colours: A: purple, bright pink, bright blue, olive
B: cream, pale pink, bright pink, grey

Method

1.   Mark out front pattern pieces on soie sauvage.

A: paint all over – areas of bright blue and pink using a cotton wool pad or a large brush. Dry thoroughly. Heat the wax and using a fan-shaped wax brush whisk over the surface at random, forming half-moon shapes. Mix up a large amount of olive green as this will be your lining colour too. Paint over waxed silk with the olive dye. Leave to dry with dots of dye remaining on the surface of the wax. Iron off wax. Fix as normal.

B: paint pale cream and pinks all over the background using a cotton wool pad or a large brush. Dry thoroughly. Heat the wax and use a fan-shaped wax brush to make circles all over the silk. Do this lightly. Mix up pale grey dye and paint over the wax. Dry carefully with a hair dryer.

Heat up the wax again. Re-apply circles all over the silk in the spaces and overlapping some of the original ones. Mix up a large amount of strong grey dye (this will also be your lining colour). Paint over the waxed silk with the grey dye and wipe off some of the excess dots of dye with cotton wool. Remove wax and fix as normal.

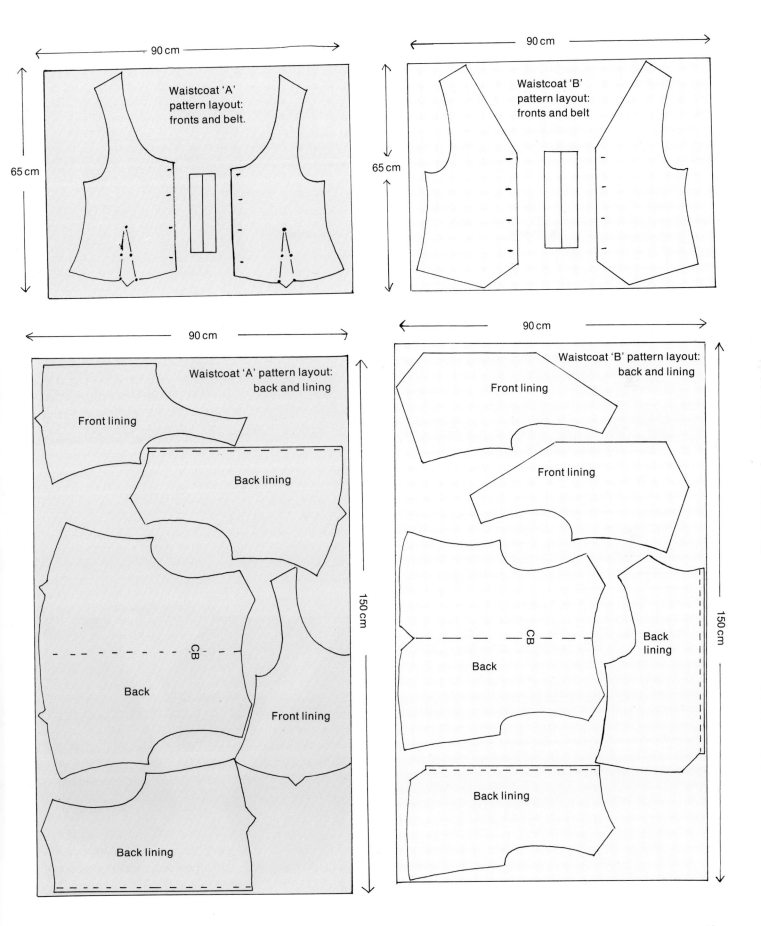

Waistcoat 'A'
pattern layout:
fronts and belt.

Waistcoat 'B'
pattern layout:
fronts and belt

90 cm

65 cm

Waistcoat 'A' pattern layout:
back and lining

Front lining

Back lining

Back

CB

Front lining

Back lining

150 cm

90 cm

Waistcoat 'B' pattern layout:
back and lining

Front lining

Front lining

Back

CB

Back
lining

Back lining

150 cm

Finished back of waistcoat

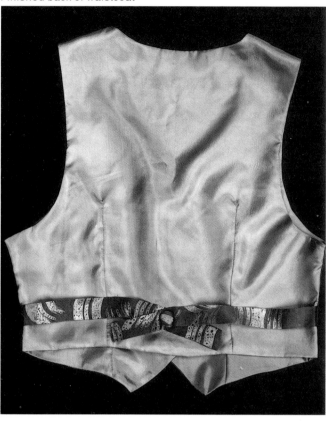

2. Paint the back and lining of waistcoats. Ours are plain, but they can be shaded or salted for extra interest. Fix as normal.

Sewing up the garments 'A' and 'B'

1. Cut out the front pieces and two belt pieces in soie sauvage. Cut out the backs and lining pieces from the pongée.

2. Waistcoat 'A'. Sew darts in fronts and lining fronts.

3. Waistcoats 'A' and 'B'. Place interfacing on wrong side of waistcoat fronts.

4. Sew two belt strips right sides together and across one end. Turn through and press. Tack to the outside seams of waistcoat front.

5. Continue following the 'grapes waistcoat' method nos. 3–6 on page 77.

6. Cover buttons to match in the leftover pieces of soie sauvage. There should also be enough for brooches and earrings; maybe even a hair bow. Work four buttonholes on the right fronts. Sew buttons on the left fronts. Sew a button on the overlapping back belt pieces.

7. Press the garment.

TIES and BOW TIES

A man's appearance can be made more individual by a silk-painted tie. It is often easier to co-ordinate with his existing wardrobe because you may choose your own colour combinations.

We have some samples here painted on soie sauvage (wild silk) which show you a wide variety of techniques and colour combinations. We recommend that you choose a strong, firm silk such as soie sauvage or a good heavy quality of crêpe de Chine. Bear in mind that the creases formed by the knot could spoil a tie made of a lighter weight of silk. We also suggest that the tie is dry cleaned so as not to reduce the 'body' of the fabric.

Designing your tie

Any pattern can be painted on a tie: stripes, dots, dashes, abstract designs. The main point to remember is that the

Close up of tie ends showing textures

tie must be cut out on the cross so that it will fold and hang properly. When planning the design, take this into consideration. On our pattern layout we show the centre front position of the tie so that you can even work out where an individual motif or signature would need to go.

Another point to consider is that one tie will be cut out from the bottom left-hand corner of silk, but the other tie will be cut from the top right-hand corner. If you are painting one motif regularly over the whole silk, then the right-hand tie might end up with a motif upside down. Try to create a motif that has no top or bottom; or one that can be painted in both directions. Stripes are ideal as they can be painted along the horizontal so when cut out they form the diagonal stripe down the tie. You can draw a gutta line down the diagonal of the silk and paint two different ties, one on each side.

Painting your tie

As you can see from the variety of effects we have created, ties can look very individual. The techniques used here are:

watercolour

wax

salt

You could also use gutta in combination with the above methods, although you must take care with a thick fabric like soie sauvage that the gutta penetrates the whole way through. You may need to gutta on the back of the silk, as well.

PROJECTS

1. **Watercolour stripe** *(see page 82)* Stretch up your silk. Choose two colours; here we have selected a bright red and grey, but any combinations can be used. Taking a narrow and a wide brush, paint evenly across the horizontal width of the silk, starting from the top. Try to blend the edge of the next colour into the one above. Work smoothly and quickly so that each band does not have time to dry out. Alternate the widths of the stripes to add interest when the tie is cut out.

2. **Salted stripe** *(see page 82)* Four colours were chosen – pale and dark grey, burgundy red and navy blue. This time the tie was painted in two stages. The pale grey, dark grey and burgundy were painted in stripes as above. As they were painted, sea salt was sprinkled randomly on the silk to create a texture when it dried. To create more interest, the fourth colour, navy, was very lightly painted over the top of the original stripes with a fine brush when the first layer was dry.

3. **Peacock feathers** *(see page 82)* The techniques used here are wax and watercolour. Two shades of jade green and emerald green were painted on the whole background area of the silk, using a large brush. The colours were painted at random but blended in where they joined. The background was then dried thoroughly and the wax heated. The heads of the feathers and spines were painted on using a fine wax brush. Make sure that your design has the heads of the feathers quite close together and in different positions so that when the tie is made up they can be seen.

The wax will have retained all of the background colour. Now simply paint over the whole piece of silk with a dark colour (we have used black). If you want a crisp, clear effect, wipe off any surplus dots of dye which may be resting on the wax with cotton wool. Sometimes it is nice to leave these on as they create extra texture: the choice is yours. When the painting is dry, iron off the wax and steam fix as instructed.

Bow ties showing wax and watercolour textures ▶

Ties showing different techniques: grey (salted), peacock (waxed) and striped (watercolour)

Making up a tie

Material used: Painted silk
                     Interlining for the centre of the tie
                     Matching lining for the end sections
Extra materials: Matching thread

Method

1.   Place the pattern pieces for one tie on the silk. It is sometimes easier to draw the layout on using a ruler and marker pen. The tie is made up of three sections cut on the bias (see Figure c).

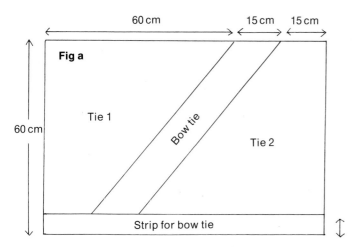

Fig a Pattern layout for two ties and one bow tie

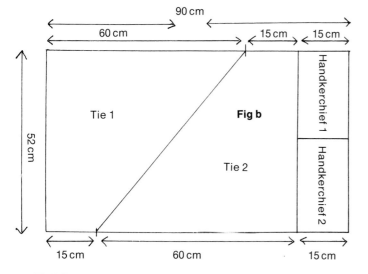

Fig b Pattern layout for two ties and two small handkerchiefs

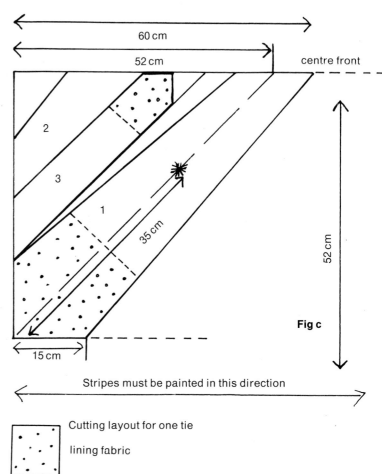

Stripes must be painted in this direction

Cutting layout for one tie

lining fabric

* Top of motif 35 cm from point.

2.   Pin the sections together numbers 1, 2 and 3 using a 1 cm ($\frac{3}{4}$ in) seam allowance. Machine and press the joins open.

3.   Cut out the centre interlining piece (see below). This can be made of any pre-shrunk woven fabric of a firm body. Tack into position down the centre of the tie.

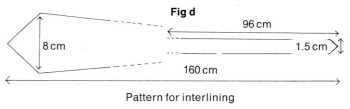

Pattern for interlining

4.   Cut out, in the lining fabric, the two lining end sections (see the spotted shading on Figure c). Tack on to the tie ends right sides together and machine carefully around the points. Trim across the points and turn through to the right side. Press the points carefully.

5. Press under 1 cm ($\frac{3}{8}$ in) down the length of one side of the tie.

6. Fold over the top of the other side and loosely slipstitch the edges together. Take care that these stitches do not penetrate through to the front.

7. Lightly press with this seam down the centre back of the tie.

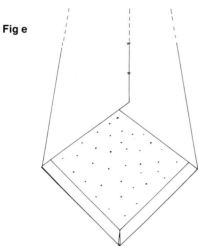

Fig e

Back of tie showing lining

Making up a bow tie

Bow ties are very fashionable at the moment, both for evening and for day wear. They tend to vary in size as fashion dictates.

The instructions given below and overleaf are for two small evening bow ties. You could allow extra material for making up a bow tie while making ordinary ties (see Figure a).

Pieces required for making the blunt-ended bow tie

BLUNT-ENDED BOW TIE

Final size: 30 cm × 30 cm (12 in × 12 in)
Material used: Painted silk cut in the following measurements:
Bow – 2 pieces 10 cm × 23 cm (4 in × 9$\frac{1}{4}$ in) cut on the bias
Knot – 1 piece 6 cm × 7 cm (2$\frac{1}{2}$ in × 2$\frac{3}{4}$ in) cut on the straight
Neckband – 1 piece 45 cm × 5 cm (18 in × 2 in) cut on the straight
Interfacing (if using soft silk) 2 pieces 4 cm × 23 cm (1$\frac{1}{2}$ in × 9$\frac{1}{4}$ in)
Extra materials: Matching thread
Velcro fastening – 4 cm (1$\frac{1}{2}$ in)

Method

1. Place interfacing down the centre of the two bow sections. Press the edges of the silk over the interfacing. Oversew the join lightly using large stitches.

2. Fold bow pieces into three, making the upper bow very slightly smaller than the lower one.

3. Machine the long neckband right sides together 1 cm ($\frac{3}{8}$ in) from the edge. Turn through to the right side. Press with the seam down the middle. Tuck under the ends and slipstitch.

4. Attach a small strip of Velcro fastening to the wrong side at one end and the right side at the other end.

5. Take the knot piece and press under 1 cm ($\frac{3}{8}$ in) on both of the long sides. Fold almost in half, enclosing the raw edges, and press again. It will be quite effective if when sewn together, the knot shows two little edges on the right side.

6. Pinch the bow sections together in the middle and hand sew securely.

7. Place the neckband behind the bows and fold the knot piece over these. Try to hold the centre tight while you overlap the back of the knot. Hand stitch neatly.

POINTED BOW TIE

Final size: 40 cm × 30 cm (16 in × 12 in)

Material used: Painted silk cut in the following measurements:
Bow – 2 pieces 6 cm × 40 cm ($2\frac{1}{2}$ in × 16 in) – cut on the bias, pointed at both ends
Knot – 1 piece 6 cm × 7 cm ($2\frac{1}{2}$ in × $2\frac{3}{4}$ in) – cut on the straight
Neckband – 1 piece 5 cm × 55 cm (2 in × 22 in) – cut on the straight

Extra materials: Matching thread
Velcro fastening – narrow stip 15 cm (6 in) narrow strip
Metal hook and ring for fastening

Method

1. Place the two pointed sections right sides together. Machine 1 cm ($\frac{3}{8}$ in) from the edge. Leave a small gap for turning in the centre of one side. Trim at the points.

2. Turn through to the right side. Press carefully.

3. Machine a narrow strip of hook Velcro 5 cm (2 in) long to the neckband silk approximately 2 cm ($\frac{3}{4}$ in) in from the long edge (see below). Machine the narrow fluffy strip of Velcro on to the silk at least 10 cm (4 in) away from the first strip and approximately 10 cm (4 in) long.

4. Machine the long neckband right sides together 1 cm ($\frac{3}{8}$ in) from the edge. Turn through. Press with the seam on the edge.

5. Tuck under one end and slipstitch in place. On the other end insert the metal hook facing uppermost.

6. Slide the metal hook into position between the two Velcro sections. The neckband is now complete.

7. Take the knot piece and press under 1 cm ($\frac{3}{8}$ in) on both the long sides. Fold almost in half, enclosing the raw edges. Press again.

8. Concertina fold the bow so that one point sits from right and the back point is back left.

9. Complete as from stage 6 on page 85.

Pieces required for making the pointed bow tie

CRAVATS and HANDKERCHIEFS

These can be painted on a softer fabric: a crêpe de Chine or twill would be suitable. The cravat below can be cut out on the straight grain if fabric is short, but hangs better if cut on the bias.

Material used: Painted silk for the front and back, *or* silk front and lining back
40 cm × 90 cm (18 in × 36 in) – if cut on the straight grain.

Cravat pattern layout

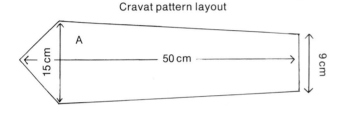

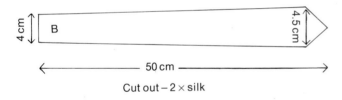

Cut out – 2 × silk

Add 1.5 cm seam allowance.

Method

1. Cut out two 'A' pieces and two 'B' pieces. (One set will be the lining.)

2. Place right sides together on both sections and machine 1 cm ($\frac{3}{8}$ in) from the edge around the point, leaving the straight narrow end open. Turn through to the right side and press.

3. Tuck under 1 cm ($\frac{3}{8}$ in) on the narrow edge of piece 'B'. Press.

4. Gather up the wide straight end of piece 'A' and push into the end of piece 'B'. Arrange the gathers neatly.

5. Either machine across this join to secure, or hand sew invisibly.

Cravats with top pocket handkerchiefs

Top pocket handkerchiefs

These are a bit of fun to link up the tie with a suit. Using the leftover end sections of silk, cut out a rectangle and neaten the raw edges with either a straight stitch or a small zigzag stitch (see Figure b on page 84).

Ladies' handkerchiefs

Painted on a fine pongée no. 7 or no. 9, handkerchiefs could make pretty, personal gifts. They are squares of silk 45 cm × 45 cm (18 in × 18 in) which when hemmed form a square of 40 cm × 40 cm (16 in × 16 in). Four handkerchiefs could be painted at one time on a 90 cm × 90 cm (36 in × 36 in) square of silk.

The handkerchiefs could include a person's name or be painted to match a special outfit and worn in a jacket pocket. Even children could paint a special one for a granny or aunt.

Ladies' floppy bows

Brighten up the neckline or collar of a plain blouse with a bow tie. Floppy bows are best made in crêpe de Chine, but other soft silk fabric could be used. We paint several at one time. The length needs to be 1.5 cm ($\frac{3}{4}$ in) and the width of each strip 20 cm (8 in). When machining up you can either form a point at the ends or sew straight across.

Home Furnishings

Pictures

Any one of the techniques for painting on silk can be used to create an original picture for your walls. If you combine a few of the techniques, you will find you have created something truly personal and unique. Even a beginner can produce work to be proud of, from miniatures to large abstract paintings which will look wonderful on your walls.

Always sign your work; this can be done in gutta or wax, or alternatively a gold or silver permanent marker can be used.

Once you have completed your silk painting and decided you would like to display it on a wall, you must decide how to present it. There are several methods of displaying your silk paintings:

- Traditional wood and metal frames
- Flat glass or perspex box frames
- Silk stapled over a wooden frame
- Wall hangings

Backing

Before mounting and framing your painting, it needs to be placed on a backing. We find a piece of cardboard or mount board ideal for this. Choose white board, as brown or grey will dull the colours on the silk. Another piece of card or hardboard can be used as a final backing sheet when placing the picture in the frame. For larger paintings, hardboard must be used to keep the picture rigid. The silk can be attached to the backing sheet by various methods:

1. The silk can be attached to the backing sheet using a spray adhesive. Great care must be used when doing this; if too much adhesive is applied it will soak through the silk. Hold the spray can 15–20 cm (3–4 in) away from the surface of the silk and coat with a fine spray. Place the silk gently into position on the backing sheet.

2. The silk can be stretched and taped to the backing board using masking tape or double-sided sticky tape. Again, this is easier with a smaller piece of silk; large pieces sometimes crease or wrinkle.

3. We find this method the best as it always eliminates any wrinkles, bubbles or creases that may occur. A sticky backing paper made for lampshade-making is used. The best method of sticking the silk to the sticky backing is to stretch it on a frame or a flat wooden board. Make sure it is right side down and that no wrinkles or bubbles are present. Then peel the covering off the backing and roll the paper on to the silk, sticky side down, rubbing with your hands as you go. Unpin the silk, turn over and make sure there are no bubbles on the right side.

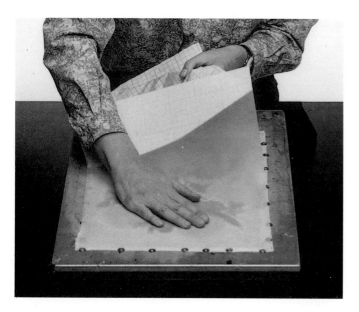

centre, which will give a similarly attractive edge.

As a general rule, good proportions when cutting mounts are 6 cm (2½ in) at the top and sides and a little more at the bottom. Obviously larger pictures can tolerate a wider mount. The mount can now be placed over the silk painting on the backing, and the picture is ready for framing.

Mounting

There are hundreds of colours to choose from when selecting your mount. Some subjects can be improved by the use of a coloured mount, but be careful and try to select a colour which will enhance your painting (see the baby picture on page 91). The purpose of a mount is to separate the painting and the glass, and to cover the edges of the silk where it has been pinned to the frame for painting.

Cut your mount board to the size of your frame. The centre piece of the mount board is then cut out, forming a window for viewing your silk. Be sure to measure and mark the rectangle on the mount board before cutting so that just the right amount of picture is showing.

A steel ruler and craft knife or an angled cutting blade are needed to cut the mount. The cutting blade is ideal for this, as a perfect 45° angle cut is obtained. However it is possible to hold your knife at an angle away from the

Framing

Traditional picture frames

Picture frames have two purposes: to protect the silk from dust and stains and to enhance the picture. The correct frame is important and can make or ruin a picture. To choose the frame for your painting, it is best to take it with you to the frame shop and try various styles. A frame that is too narrow may spoil the picture, while a frame that is too large will smother the painting. Today there is a wide choice of frames available. You can buy ready-made frames, or pre-cut self-assembly frames, or even build your own.

Ready-made frames

Ready-made frames are available in a wide choice of styles and many different sizes. It is worth checking on these before you mount your painting; if you have a difficult size you will have to build your own frame or take your picture to a professional frame-maker.

A traditionally mounted baby birthday picture (see page 96)

Pre-cut self-assembly frames

Pre-cut frames which you can easily assemble yourself are available in most art and craft shops and hardware stores. They clip or screw together at the corners. We find this method very economical if you have a few paintings to frame, are hesitant about building your own and don't want to spend a lot of money at a specialized shop. These pre-cut frames are available in wood, metal and plastic, and come in a wide variety of colours and finishes.

Two sets of lengths are required in the sizes appropriate for your painting. You will also need a piece of backing board and glass.

Building your own frame

One advantage of building your own frame is that you can decide on the exact measurements you need for your painting. If you decide to do this, it is worth investing in a mitre box so that you make accurate 45° corner cuts. A

Miniature pictures showing different techniques

set of four clamps is also a good idea, as it allows you to glue up all the frame at once.

There are hundreds of different mouldings to choose from but try to select one which will complement your painting. First saw off the end of your moulding at a 45° angle, then carefully measure the longest side of the mounted picture and add 0.25 cm ($\frac{1}{8}$ in) to this measurement to allow the silk painting to fit into the frame easily.

Measure the moulding and starting from the edge of the mitre cut at a point where the picture inserts into the frame. Mark and cut a 45° mitre at the other end of the piece you have just cut. Repeat this process, as you will need a piece exactly the same for the opposite side. Next measure the short sides of the picture and cut two pieces of moulding this length, not forgetting to add the extra 0.25 cm ($\frac{1}{8}$ in) to allow your painting to fit the frame. Now the parts are all ready to assemble.

Take one side piece and the bottom piece and coat with glue the ends which are to be joined. Place carefully in the clamps and tighten while you nail the corners together. Check that the pictures will fit the frame. Repeat this process in the other three corners and allow the glue to dry thoroughly.

Glass

When buying the glass for your frames, you will find there are two kinds: single-strength picture glass, and non-reflecting (sometimes called non-glare) glass. Perspex can also be used: it has the advantage of being much lighter in weight than glass, which can be useful in a very large painting; however, it does tend to scratch easily.

Primulas in a flat glass frame (see page 96)

To assemble the picture

Check that you have everything in the right order and the right way up, and that the glass is clean. You should have: frame, glass, picture, mount, whiteboard, hardboard.

Place everything into the frame and use brads or glass points to hold the backing in place. Insert these all around at 10 cm (4 in) intervals. The back of the frame can be sealed using brown paper. This can be taped to the frame using gummed paper or masking tape, or you can wet the brown paper before applying. As it dries it will shrink to a tight finish.

Fix some screw eyes to each side and fasten wire or heavy cord across. Your silk painting is now ready to hang and enjoy.

Flat glass or perspex box frames

These are very easy to use. Perspex box frames can look particularly effective with a silk painting inside, as you can see through the sides and do not need a mount. Flat glass frames, sometimes called poster frames, can be used with a mount or you can display your silk painting using spray adhesive and the frayed edge look (see p. 40).

Staple the silk over a wooden frame

This is an inexpensive method for framing your silk. The silk is stapled around a wooden frame and backed with a cotton lining to strengthen it. This has the same appearance as the perspex box in that you can see the sides of the painting, but has the disadvantage of giving no protection from glass or perspex so that in time your painting will get dusty and may stain and fade in the sun. If you have padded, quilted and beaded your silk picture, this is an ideal way to display it as the effect you have created may be lost if you put it behind glass.

Wall hangings

Wall hangings can be supported by a pole which runs through a casing. This is formed by sewing approximately 3 cm ($1\frac{1}{4}$ in) away from the top edge of the

Materials required to assemble and hang your picture

Domes in a perspex box, 40 × 60 cm (16 in × 24 in)

hanging. Sew the layers of fabric together with small running stitches. Turn under the fabric ends and sew by hand to finish off. Then simply slide the pole through the opening formed. Attach the pole to the wall with hooks.

The base of the wall hanging can be held together by two wooden battens. These are glued together using a rubber-based glue with the layers of fabric sandwiched in between. The battens need clamping firmly until the glue dries. An alternative method is to simply turn under the lower edges and sew together neatly by hand. Weights can be inserted before sewing to make your work hang evenly.

Stapling silk and lining around a wooden frame

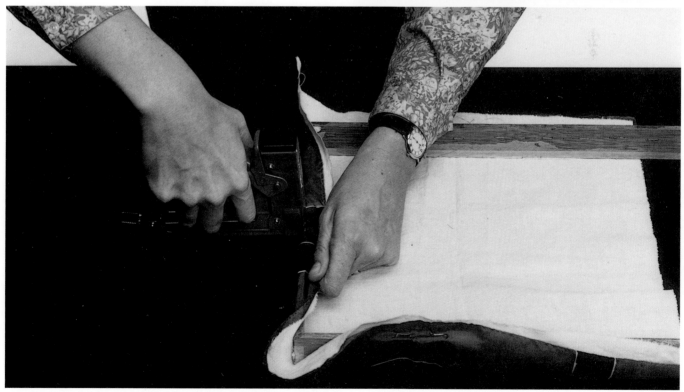

painted using brown dye diluted to a pale beige with diluent. Paint the leaves and flowers using a variety of reds and greens to create interesting shading effects. After fixing, remove the wax by ironing (remember not to dry clean the silk as this will remove the gold gutta). This picture has a backing layer of white cotton and has been stapled over a wooden frame.

Quilted flower wall hanging (see page 96)

CHRISTMAS WREATH

Material used: Silk pongée no. 9
Dimensions: Cut your silk 75 cm × 90 cm
(30 in × 36 in)
Finished picture 60 cm × 75 cm
(24 in × 30 in)
Technique: Wax and gutta (gold), no. 5 nib
Colours: Brown, red and green

Method
After drawing the wreath on the silk, the delicate white flowers are painted using molten wax and a thin brush. Gold gutta is then used to outline all the flowers, berries, leaves, etc. When the gutta is dry, the background can be

EDELWEISS FLOWER SHOP

Material used: Silk pongée no. 9
Dimensions: 90 cm × 60 cm (36 in × 30 in)
Technique: Wax, antifusant
Colours: Red, green, yellow, blue, purple, orange

Method

This painting uses a combination of wax and antifusant techniques. When painting either traditional or false batik it is very difficult to obtain reds and greens on the same painting without a long process whereby the picture must be dry cleaned and re-waxed halfway through the work. Here, by covering the silk with a solution of antifusant, many coloured flowers can be painted directly on to the silk. Wax any flowers, pots, lables, etc. which are to remain white, and then wax over all the coloured flower heads you have painted. The work then continues as a false batik, waxing and drying as many times as you wish. Finally, remove the wax by ironing and dry cleaning or by soaking in white spirit. Wash and iron the silk; cut a mount and frame using one of the methods shown earlier. We chose to use a sticky backing on this picture (see page 89).

QUILTED FLOWER WALL HANGING

See finished design on page 94

Material used: 3 m (3¼ yds) crêpe de Chine
1.5 m (1¾ yd) lining
1.5 m (1¾ yd) wadding
Dimensions: 85 cm × 140 cm (34 in × 56 in)
Cut silk 90 cm × 150 cm (36 in × 60 in)
Technique: Gutta (black), watercolour, salt, alcohol, antifusant
Colours: Beige, purple, orange, red, brown, grey

Method

The design for the wall hanging is loosely based on a flower. Half of the silk area will form the front of the wall hanging, hay will form the back. The design was sketched lightly on to the front of the wall hanging and grew as the paint was applied.

The gutta lines in black were drawn as an indication of the design, but were not intended to inhibit the progression of the painting.

The background is painted first. In order to get an even wash, paint the silk in diluent. Using very muted tones of beige, orange, grey and brown cover the whole background area. Sprinkle a little sea salt in selected areas to create a texture. Dry.

Strong tones for the leaves, stems and hillsides can now be painted in using grey, brown, tan and cinnamon colours. Allow the dyes to creep over the silk to create interesting shapes. Halt the movement by drying them quickly with a hair dryer.

Continue to fill in the trumpet-shaped flower heads using purple and many tones of red. Dry and repaint to create decorative outlines. When the basic shape has been painted, dry thoroughly. Coat the flower area and its surround with antifusant (see page 29). Now you can paint further delicate colours on top of the initial ones to create more depth in your work. These will show up much stronger when the silk is fixed.

Paint the back of the hanging in pale cream, tan and grey tones to link up with the front. Quilt selected areas (see page 71) and complete the hanging as on pages 92 and 93.

BABY'S BIRTHDAY PICTURE

See finished design on page 91

Material used: Silk pongée no. 9
Dimensions: 80 cm × 65 cm (32 in × 26 in)
Technique: Gutta (gold), no. 6 nib
Colours: Iron-on dyes: white, red, yellow, blue, green, purple

Method

Draw the design on to the silk and outline using gold gutta and a no. 6 nib. When the gutta is dry, paint using iron-on dyes. A white dye is available which can be mixed with other colours to obtain lovely pastel shades. When fixed, the picture can be stuck on a sticky backing (see page 89), mounted using blue mount board, and framed in a traditional wooden frame.

PRIMULAS IN A BASKET

See finished design on page 91

Material used: Silk pongée no. 9
Dimensions: 60 cm × 50 cm (24 in × 24 in)
Technique: Gutta (gold), no. 5 nib
Colours: Brown, orange, red, green, yellow

Method

This is a straightforward gutta painting. Try to create shading on the basket and leaves. When painting the flowers, add a second colour while the first is still wet to obtain the distinctive primula look.

When the painting has been fixed, carefully tear down each side and then fray the edges. Spray the back with adhesive and stick on the mount board before framing in a flat glass frame.

LUPINS IN A VASE and FIELD OF SUNFLOWERS

See finished designs on page 98
Material used: Silk pongée no. 9
Dimensions: Lupins in a vase – 70 cm × 90 cm
(28 in × 36 in)
Colours: Pink, red, maroon, brown, olive green, black
Field of sunflowers – 85 cm × 70 cm
(34 in × 28 in)
Colours: Yellow, olive, salad green, brown, black
Technique: False batik

Method

These two pictures have both been painted using the false batik method described on page 24.

NEW YORK SKYLINE

See finished design on page 99
Material used: Silk pongée no. 9
Dimensions: Cut your silk 90 cm × 45 cm
(36 in × 18 in)
Finished picture 85 cm × 40 cm
(34 in × 16 in)
Technique: Gutta (clear), no. 5 nib
Colours: Blue, grey and pink

Method

Draw your design on the silk, and use a no. 5 nib and clear gutta to outline all the buildings. When the gutta is dry, paint the sky in any combinations of colours you like – sunsets, stormy clouds and night skies can all be attempted as backgrounds. Proceed by painting all the buildings and the river in tones of grey and blue. After fixing the silk is washed, ironed and mounted on a sticky backing (see page 89) before framing.

ABSTRACT

See finished design on page 99
Material used: 90 cm × 90 cm (36 in × 36 in) Crêpe de Chine
Dimensions: 80 cm × 80 cm (32 in × 32 in)
Technique: Salt, spray, antifusant
Colours: Turquoise, green, blue, purple, red

Method

Drawing shapes on the silk is not necessary, but you must have a firm idea of the picture design before starting to paint.

The background is first sprayed in pale jade and green. The silk is then coated with antifusant – this may need a second coat when used on crêpe de Chine. The stronger colours are then painted on the silk and salt applied sparingly to create texture on the left-hand side.

When dry, some areas are overpainted to create further dimensions.

Lupins in a vase

Field of sunflowers

Abstract

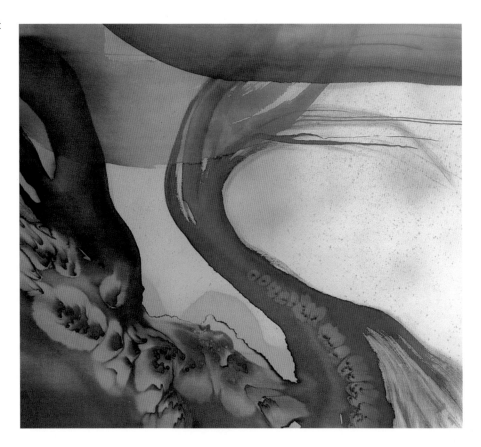

New York skyline

COT QUILT

A rocking horse design and delicate pastel shades are used on this pretty cot quilt. The finished design can be seen on page 102.

Material used: Silk pongée no. 9 145 cm × 190 cm (56½ in × 75 in)
Wadding 110 cm × 140 cm (44 in × 56 in)
Backing material

Technique: The rocking horse squares were all painted separately; however, time can be saved by painting four at once on a frame. The dyes on the rocking horse quilt are the iron-on variety, in which a white is available, making lovely pastel shades possible. A long frame is needed to paint the border pieces. Again these can all be painted on one frame.

Colours: Pastel blue, pink, yellow, green

Method

Cut 12 single squares 35 cm × 35 cm (14 in × 14 in) allowing for hems, or three 70 cm × 70 cm (28 in × 28 in) allowing for squares to be painted at once. Paint your design in a 30 cm × 30 cm (12 in × 12 in) box in the middle of the squares. Paint the border strips; you will need 6 lengths as shown in the diagram below.

When all the silk has been painted and fixed, the squares need to be sewn together, taking care to match the edges and corners. Sew the three outer borders around the squares. Add the wadding and backing material and quilt (see page 71).

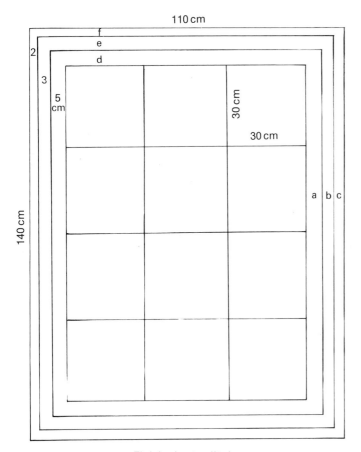

Finished cot quilt size

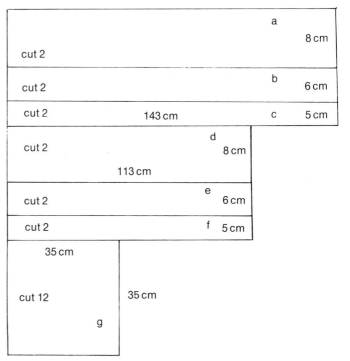

Pattern pieces for cot quilt

Silk cushions give the impression of something rather fragile and delicate, but are in fact surprisingly strong and versatile, depending upon the weight of silk used and their position within a room scheme. As floor cushions with regular use, they certainly would not last very long, but on sofas, window recesses, or piled in masses on beds or chairs, they can create wonderful effects. Try to place informal shapes and sizes together, maybe linked by a similar motif or toning colour (see the picture of the boudoir cushions, on page 103.)

This section shows a large variety of silk painting techniques combined with many ways of constructing and completing the cushions. Once again we hope that these will give you the opportunity to put your ideas into practice.

Cushion pads

The easiest way to decide on cushion sizes is to paint your silk according to the size of the cushion pad. These are now available in many different sizes and with a variety of fillings. Failing this, you can use one of a number of loose fillings which can be put into a similar-sized casing. Old feather cushions can be recycled; try damping the old cushion with water and then putting it into the tumble dryer until the feathers are dry and fluffy. When putting feathers into a new casing keep the doors and windows closed if indoors, alternatively on a calm day, do it outside.

Suggested pad sizes:

30 cm × 30 cm (12 in × 12 in)   very small square
35 cm × 35 cm (14 in × 14 in)   medium square
40 cm × 40 cm (16 in × 16 in)   standard cushion size
45 cm × 45 cm (18 in × 18 in)   old English square size
90 cm × 90 cm (36 in × 36 in)   floor cushion
40 cm (16 in) across   heart
appropriate size   bolster

The pads are available in feather and down, and synthetic fibres. Feather pads are best for silk cushions, as they seem to give weight and elegance; they also 'plump up' well.

Stuffings are also available in a variety of forms, although the cheaper foam chips really do not look as nice. Try to obtain a good quality acrylic or polyester wadding for a smooth filling. A normal 40 cm × 40 cm (16 in × 16 in) cushion should take approximately 600 g (21 oz) of fibre filling.

Rose cushion with lace insert

Fabrics

Most of our samples here use pongée no. 10, which we find is strong and withstands a fair amount of wear. We have also used pongée no. 9 and crêpe de Chine. Wild silk is also ideal for painted tones and colours, although it is rather stiff for frills.

The cushions are all lined to give extra strength. In the case of the paler cushions, a white lining underneath the silk shows off their subtle colours to a greater advantage. We use nylon lining as it will not shrink and is strong. Fine cotton can also be used, but must be pre-shrunk before being made up into cushions. The linings are mounted on the silk and the results are used as one fabric rather than inserted separately.

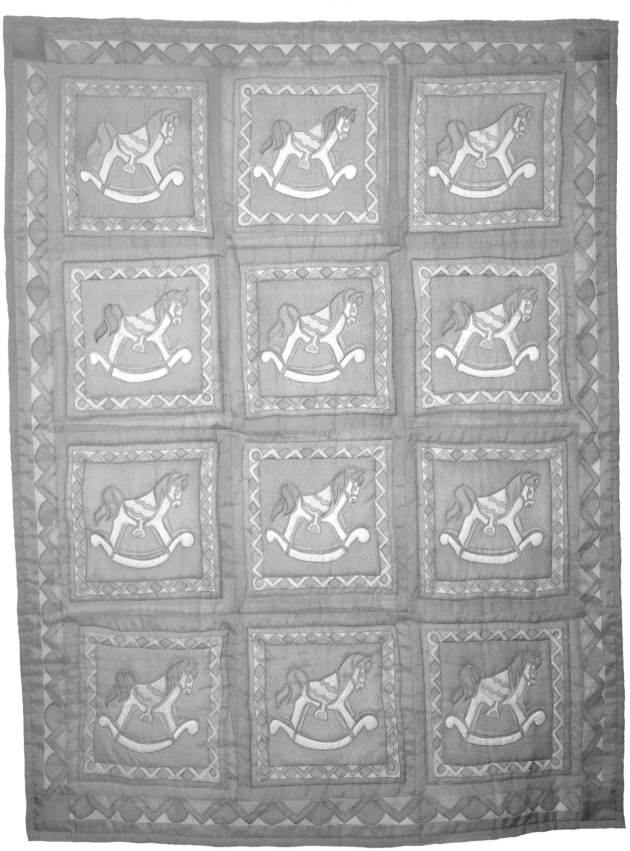

Cot quilt painted in squares then assembled

Boudoir cushions using various silk painting techniques and with a variety of edge finishes

Estimating fabric

Once the cushion pad has been chosen or the final size decided upon, use a tape measure to calculate the size of the cushion cover, which should be the same size as the cushion plus the turnings, which need to be 5 cm (2 in) extra. This will give each seam 2.5 cm (1 in) extra. This will enable you to paint your silk comfortably and in the construction you will be able to cut away any unwanted pin marks or painting problems. If you are painting more than one cushion with a similar design, it is sensible to paint at least two at a time so that the colours will match. From a 90 cm × 90 cm (36 in × 36 in) square you can paint two 40 cm × 40 cm (16 in × 16 in) square cushions (see diagram).

Here are approximate suggestions of fabric sizes for individual cushions. There are many commercial patterns available these days with interesting cushion features, which are highly recommended.

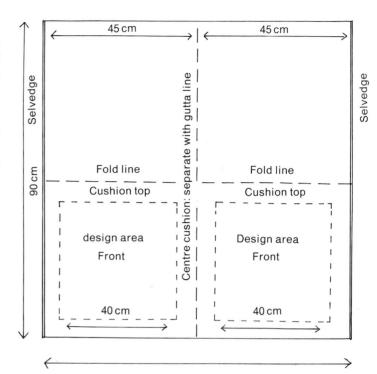

	Final size	**Fabric**
Square	30 cm × 30 cm (12 in × 12 in)	35 cm × 70 cm (14 in × 28 in)
	35 cm × 35 cm (14 in × 14 in)	40 cm × 80 cm (16 in × 32 in)
	40 cm × 40 cm (16 in × 16 in)	45 cm × 90 cm (18 in × 36 in)
	90 cm × 90 cm (36 in × 36 in)	95 cm × 190 cm (38 in × 76 in)
Round	35 cm (14 in) diameter	40 cm × 80 cm (16 in × 32 in)
	40 cm (16 in) diameter	45 cm × 90 cm (18 in × 36 in)

Heart	See diagram below	
	40 cm × 50 cm (16 in × 20 in)	60 cm × 90 cm (24 in × 37 in)

Bolster	See diagram below
	100 cm × 35 cm diameter (40 in × 14 in)

All extras such as frills and contrasting pipings should be calculated separately. These will be discussed in detail on pages 108 and 109.

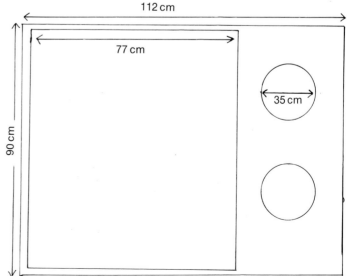

Layout for round bolster – contrast pleated frill needed

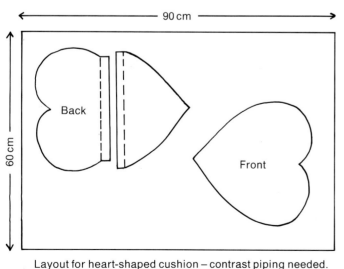

Layout for heart-shaped cushion – contrast piping needed.

Fastenings

The method of finishing off a cushion needs to be considered before it is painted. The following need no further addition of fabric; slipstitch finish, side seam zip insertion, side seam Velcro insertion, press-stud tape. **Note:** when a closure is required in the centre back of a cushion rather than at the edge, *an extra 5–6 cm (2–2½ in) of fabric is needed* on the back piece for the turnings (see heart-shape diagram opposite, below).

Methods of fastening

● *Slipstitch*

Allow an opening no less than 10 cm (4 in) shorter than one side of the cushion. Insert the pad and, using a matching thread, slipstitch the edges invisibly together closing the hole. The disadvantage of this method is that the cover will need to be unpicked and re-sewn every time the cushion is washed.

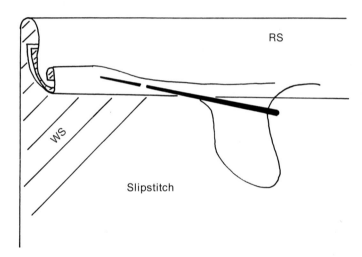

Slipstitch

● *Zip fastening*

This method is neat and ideal for silk cushions. Place right sides of fabric together. Tack along the seam line and press open. Place the zip face down on the tacked seam line. Machine down the centre of the tape, and to the ends of the cushion. Neaten inside the seam allowance. Oversew neatly from the end of the zip tape to the cushion edge to join up the seam.

Inserting zip: edge to edge method

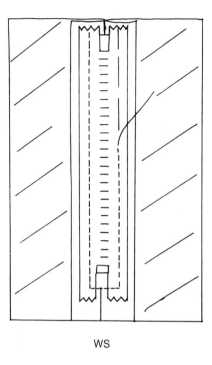

WS

Place zip right side down on opening then tack and machine in place

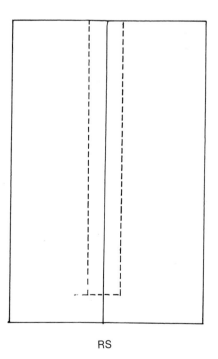

RS

Zip in position

● *Ties*

For this technique, extra matching or contrasting fabric will need to be painted. Cut out at least 4 ties for a 40 cm × 40 cm (16 in × 16 in) cushion (less for a smaller one). The width of the ties can vary according to taste: a final size of 2 cm ($\frac{3}{4}$ in) would require a strip of 10 cm (4 in). The length can also vary, but a minimum length of 25 cm (10 in) for each side is necessary. Therefore 100 cm ($39\frac{1}{2}$ in) of fabric would be needed for your ties. Press under 1 cm ($\frac{3}{8}$ in) towards the centre on both edges of the tie strips. Fold in half and machine along the edge turning under the ends neatly. Position on cushion on both side edges of the opening. Machine neatly in place along the length of the seam.

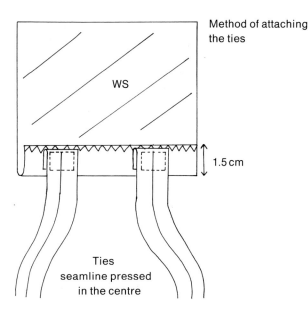

Method of attaching the ties

WS

1.5 cm

Ties seamline pressed in the centre

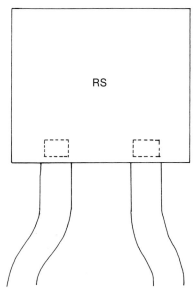

RS

● *Strip/press-stud fastening*

These methods can be attached by hand and are very strong; however, they are rather bulky for silk cushions. Turn under the seam allowances. Tack each Velcro strip or fastening to the opposite edges of the cushion opening as shown below. Make sure that the overlap will face the back of the cushion so that the opening does not show. Machine stitch neatly in place. Construct cushion.

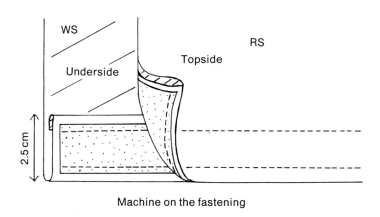

WS

Underside

RS

Topside

2.5 cm

Machine on the fastening

Completing cushions

Square cushion

1. Iron the silk fabric flat. Lay it on an even surface. Using a fade-away marker pen draw the cutting lines (cushion size + seam allowances). Carefully cut out the pieces in silk. Cut the lining pieces to exactly the same size.

2. Tack lining and the silk together – use together as one fabric.

3. Insert fastening at this stage.

4. Place front and back pieces right sides together. Pin and tack around the remaining three sides on seam allowance: 1.5 cm ($\frac{5}{8}$ in).

5. Machine stitch. Trim seam allowances and clip the corners diagonally.

6. Zigzag raw edges to neaten.

7. Turn to right side and roll seam line to edge. Press carefully.

8. Insert cushion pad. Fill the corners and 'plump up'.

Round cushion

This can be constructed in the same way as the square cushion although a fastening should be inserted across the centre of the cushion, rather than at the curved seam edge. Always clip the seam allowance well so that a round shape is formed. See measurements on page 104.

Bolster

Two circles of silk and lining are cut out (see diagram on page 104). The central panel is a rectangle. Insert the zip down the length of the rectangle. Attach pleated frill to sew on the end circles (see page 109). Machine, clip and finish off the edges.

Fancy edgings

Silk cushions can be given many interesting edge decorations. These can be made from commercially-produced haberdashery such as lace, cords and braids, but it can make a cushion much more attractive if you add a silk painted edging. We have shown several different treatments in this chapter.

Fancy cushion edgings: piping, frilled, ruched and tied with raised pintucks

Bias binding

Bias binding
The fabric is cut on the bias to give flexibility when bent around a corner, as with the piping used on cushions.

Cutting and making the strips

1.   Fold the raw edge which is cut across the grain parallel to the selvedge. Cut strips of material of the required width following the lines shown in the diagram below. Narrow strips for piping are usually the finished width of the cord × 4 (approximately 3 cm, $1\frac{3}{16}$ in).

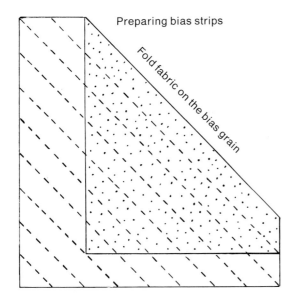

Preparing bias strips

Fold fabric on the bias grain

Cut strips along parallel lines

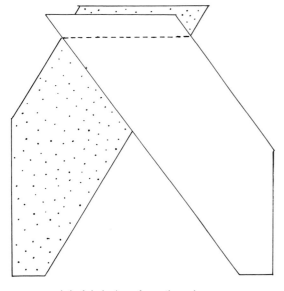

Join fabric 1 cm from the edges

2.   Join the seams to make a continuous strip. A flat seam of 1 cm ($\frac{3}{8}$ in) is usual along the straight grain (see diagram below, left). Press seams open and clip off corners.

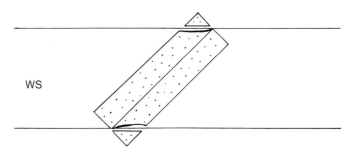

WS

Press seam open and clip off corners

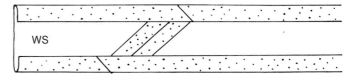

WS

Bias strips showing turnings

Piping
This decorative edge is often used in soft furnishing to add a contrast and professional look to a cushion or quilt.

 The fabric strip is cut on the bias and moulded around a cord. The cord is usually of white cotton synthetic fibre. Always boil cotton cord to shrink it before use, otherwise you could end up with puckered cushions.

Making the piping

1.   Cut and prepare the bias strip. Do not press the turnings under.

2.   Lay the cord down the centre of the wrong side of the bias strip and fold in half.

3.   Tack the two sides of the fabric together close to the cord.

4.   Machine the fabric using a zip foot so that the cord is tightly trapped inside the fabric.

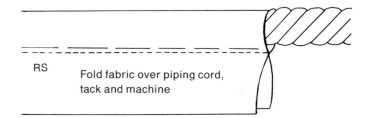

RS   Fold fabric over piping cord, tack and machine

Using the piping

The piping is sewn into the seamline.

1.   Sandwich the piping in between the right sides of the outer fabric.

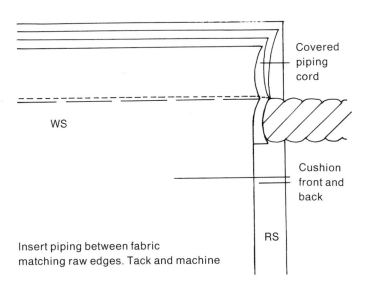

Insert piping between fabric matching raw edges. Tack and machine

2.   Tack close to piping and machine. Try to round the corners of a cushion slightly so that the piping forms an even curve. It may be easier to tack the piping in place on one right side of a cushion first, then tack the second on top.

3.   Trim seam allowances to reduce the bulk.

4.   Turn and press.

Ruched piping

This is a fancy decorative edging for cushions.

1.   Cut and make a bias strip double the width of the cord to be covered and two and a half times the length needed.

2.   Lay the piping cord in the centre of the wrong side of the fabric. Tack 1 cm ($\frac{3}{8}$ in) away from the cord so that it is loose inside.

3.   Gather the bias strip evenly as you tack so that the cord is covered by ruched fabric.

4.   Insert as usual.

Frills

These can be any width, but as silk is so fine it is better to make them double the fabric width plus the seam allowances.

The silk can be evenly gathered or pleated (see diagram below).

Cut the fabric on the straight grain for gathered frills. If enough fabric is available, cut the strips on the bias for pleated frills, which gives a better effect.

Decorative finishes on the surface of cushions

Use your silk painting as a basis for various decorative treatments to the surface of your cushions. The examples shown in this section include a wide variety of techniques, some more complicated than others, but all giving interesting effects: lace insertions, pin tucking on the diagonal, machine Italian quilting, machine embroidery.

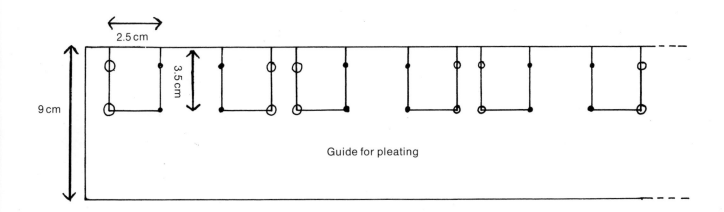

Guide for pleating

PROJECTS

KNOT CUSHIONS

Finished size: 40 cm × 40 cm (16 in × 16 in)
Material used: Pongée no. 9
Dimensions: 2 pieces 90 cm × 90 cm (36 in × 36 in)
Technique: Gutta
Colours: Red, blue, yellow, green

Method
The effect of these four cushions is created by the juxtaposition of the colours within the set. Each has a different background colour and the knot is filled in using the remaining colours. The design can be repeated on the back of the cushion, or the same background colour can be used over the whole area.

1 sq = 5 cm

ZOO ANIMAL CUSHIONS

Finished size: 40 cm × 40 cm (16 in × 16 in)
Material used: Pongée no. 10
Dimensions: 2 pieces 90 cm × 90 cm (36 in × 36 in)
Technique: Wax
Colours: Black

Method
Draw the animal motifs carefully on each cushion front. Heat the wax. Using a fine brush, cover over all the areas which are to remain white. A smooth wax outline is necessary to give a sharp contrast of colour. When it has hardened, paint over the wax with black dye. It may be necessary to put on a second coat to ensure a deep, strong colour. Dry thoroughly and iron off the wax between paper. Fix using a double layer of paper for protection.

1 sq = 5 cm

TULIP STENCIL CUSHIONS

Finished size: 40 cm × 40 cm (16 in × 16 in)
Material used: Pongée no. 10
Dimensions: 1 piece 90 cm × 45 cm (36 in × 18 in)
Technique: Spray and stencil (iron fix dyes)
Colours: Pale cream, peach, pink, turquoise,
                    green

Method

Stretch out the plain silk on a frame. Stand the frame upright and, using a mouth diffuser or spray, lightly colour the background with cream and peach dye. Do not go too close to the silk or the dyes will merge. Allow it to dry completely. Prepare the tulip stencil; using the thicker, iron-fix dyes, stipple the petals and leaves delicately with shades of peach/pink and green/turquoise. Dry thoroughly and iron on the wrong side. Steam fix the silk as normal.

1 sq = 8 cm

BLUE LACE CUSHION

Finished size: 40 cm × 40 cm (16 in × 16 in)
Material used: Pongée no. 10
Dimensions: 1 piece 90 cm × 45 cm (36 in × 18 in)
Technique: Spray
Colours: Pale blue

Method
This effect is created by stretching the plain white silk on a frame. A piece of lace curtaining is pinned over the top of the silk. Pale blue dye is then sprayed on the silk through the holes in the lace. The piece of lace is lifted away from the silk, taking care not to smudge the dyes. Once dried, the lace can be used for successive sprayings.

The blue frill is painted on a separate piece of silk but the same colour dye used.

Blue lace cushion (left) and pastel rose bolster (back). Watercolour technique is used on the heart cushion and on the lilac cushion which has a salt impregnated background

PASTEL ROSE BOLSTER

Material used: Pongée no. 10
Dimensions: 112 cm × 90 cm (44 in × 36 in)
90 cm × 90 cm (36 in × 36 in) – frill
Technique: Sugar
Colours: Pale/deep pink, pale/deep yellow, pale/mid blue

Method
See the diagram on page 104 for cutting instructions. First paint the frill, using subtle tones of pink all over the silk. Stretch the piece of silk for the sugar technique separately (see method of making syrup, on page 27). Heat the liquid. Paint bold strokes of syrup in large rose-like shapes all over the silk. Liberally paint on the three pale dye colours, keeping each colour within a rose motif. Add the stronger colours to the centres. Join all the unpainted areas with very watery colours. Do not be afraid to splash it on, but avoid painting over the syrup itself, only up to it. Add more strokes of syrup to the centres and drop it on bare patches. Leave flat to dry for one or two days. Steam sugar pieces separately from other work. Wash thoroughly to remove the sugar.

Painted silk can look wonderful as handsome lampshades. Different atmospheres can be created by choosing from a range of painting methods and by varying the colours.

Your lampshades can create charm by both day and night, reflecting the character of your room. It can also be extremely useful in linking separate colours within a room. How often have you wished that you could find a subtle and unusual lampshade in the shops? Now you can paint your own extremely personal and effective room accessories. Link the colours of the cushions and table covers with those of the lampshades and create a harmony within your room.

Types of lampshades

You must decide which shape of lampshade would suit your room, taking several conditions into account:

● The position in which it is to be situated; is it to be high up or low down?

● Is the lampshade to hang from the ceiling, or have you a specific shaped base to utilize?

● The base of the lamp will often suggest the form and the dimensions of the shade.

● Will the lampshade be mainly an effective decoration, or is it a necessary light source?

● Which shape will suit the style of your furniture?

Straight-sided drum shades suit most situations; the conical 'Chinese hat' shape often suits a 1930s style and a square or rectangular shape blends well with modern, more geometric lines.

The trend at the moment is for oval or tapered conical shades, with a smaller ring at the top. Such shades are ideal for tables, as the light bulb is not so visible from above and the design shows more effectively.

It is quite easy to renovate an existing lampshade. Simply remove the old backing from the two rings. Try not to cut into this too much, as it is the template for your new backing and shade. Clean the two rings using a little sandpaper, and you are ready to start.

Colour and design

Once the position and shape of your lampshade is decided, then the importance of the design and final effect need to be considered. Any light bulb behind the shade will allow some light through, whatever the colour, even if it is only from the top or bottom.

In most rooms the colours are extremely important, whether they are used to link or contrast with the existing ones. If the effect is to add warmth to a room, any yellows, oranges, reds, pinks, creams and light browns will add a glow. The cooler tones are citrus yellow, greens, blues, purples, greys and black. Vibrant effects can be gained by adding a touch of contrasting colour.

Your design can be simply bands of colour in stripes or gutta lines, or flowers and birds. Salt and wax effects can be striking. The pattern can be placed all over the shade or just in the centre. Our ideas in this chapter are merely suggestions of different styles that can be created to suit a variety of situations.

Try to link the design up at the back of your shade. This is not easy, as even a minor adjustment to the position of the silk on the backing can affect the final join. It is probably simpler not to have any motif or definite line by the actual join; certainly a half tree or bird would look very odd. Think carefully about the edges at this stage. The darkest and strongest colour is usually used at the base of the shade to give the final result stability; this naturally happens with landscapes. A motif in the foreground will also give the same effect.

Plan the design position carefully before drawing on the silk so that the chosen image actually shows where it is wanted. This is especially important with squares and ovals. Do not overwork your design. Once the finished shade is constructed, even simple colours and washes become incredibly effective.

Calculation

There are many shapes of lampshades available in good craft shops or furnishing stores. Sometimes it is possible to have specific sizes made up for you. If you are not sure about proportions, look at ready-made shades and take their dimensions – while no one is looking!

We prefer not to use strutted frames, as the effect of the silk in conjunction with pastel colours is often marred by the strong vertical lines which show through when the lampshade is lit. Top and bottom rings can be used with the stiff, clear, sticky parchment which is available for mounting the fabric on. This easily supports the rim and frames, and is used on all of the following lampshades: squares, oval, drum, conical, tapered conical ('Chinese hat'), and wall.

Assortment of frames for lampshades: square, oval, drum, conical and wall

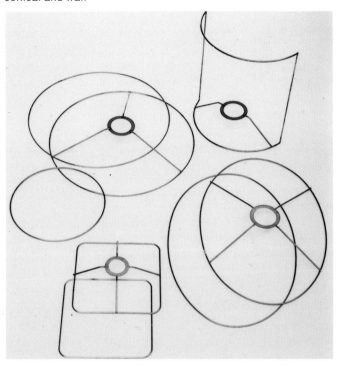

Calculating the backing

It is essential to make a template first. The following shapes are straight-sided, and therefore easier to construct.

Square, oval, drum and wall. Two frames of exactly the same diameter are needed, one of which will support the light fitting. Equipment required: ruler, paper, tape measure, pencil and card.

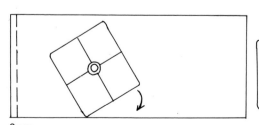

2 cm Template for square lampshade

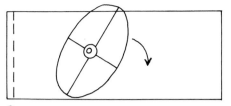

2 cm Template for oval lampshade

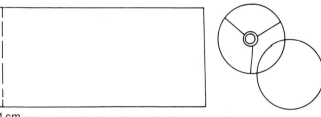

1 cm Template for drum lampshade

The backing will be an exact measurement of the perimeter of the frame or ring, plus 1–2 cm ($\frac{3}{8}$–$\frac{3}{4}$ in) for the overlap join, multiplied by the height required. This is important, as if the backing is cut too short the shade will be ruined. It is sometimes possible to trim off excess on the underside of the join if the overlap is too great, unless you are trying to get the perfect match of a design.

With the square and wall frames, remember that a little length is always lost when turning a corner; the backing does not always attach so tightly, so allow 1 cm ($\frac{3}{8}$ in) extra in length.

Conical shade. This tapered shade has a smaller ring at one end and a wider ring at the other. The different diameters of these rings vary the slope of the sides. This creates problems, which can be overcome if the construction is tackled stage by stage. The silk and backing will not be straight but will form a curve. Draw the shape using the following method:

1. Following the diagram below, measure the diameter of top ring AB, and the bottom ring CD.

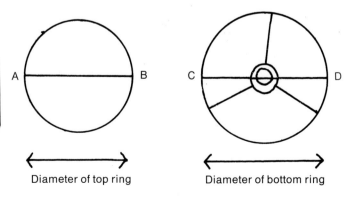

Diameter of top ring   Diameter of bottom ring

2. Decide on the distance between the upper and lower rings and measure this vertical height, EF.

3. Take a large sheet of paper, preferably plain but newspaper will do, and make a drawing of the dimensions measured, as shown in fig. 1 below. Extend AC and BD until they intersect at point G.

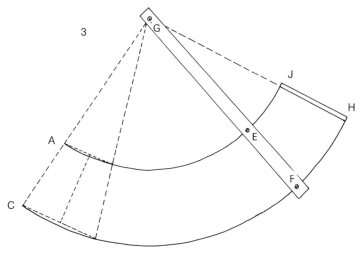

3

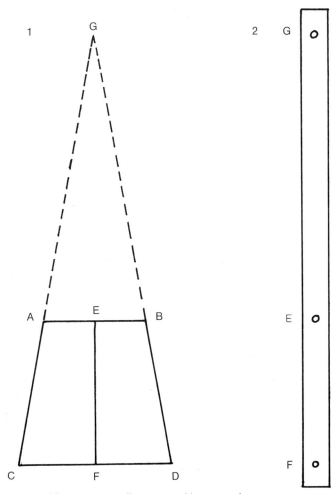

Measurement diagram and 'compass'

Making template for conical lampshade

4. Make a large 'compass' whose length is at least equal to the distance FG. This can be made from a strip of stiff card with two holes in it through which a pencil can be passed. The holes are placed corresponding to distances E and F, from G as shown in fig. 2 above. (An alternative is simply to use a piece of string with a pencil tied at one end.)

5. Fix one end of the 'compass' at G using a pin. Ensuring that the pivot at point G does not move, trace two arcs corresponding to the top and bottom of the lampshade (see fig. 3).

6. Measure the circumference of the bottom ring (it is possible to calculate this dimension by multiplying the diameter by $\frac{22}{7}$ or 3.14).

7. Take a piece of string and measure a length equal to this circumference.

8. Fix one end at C; lay the string around the bottom arc and mark off the correct length CH.

9. Repeat steps 6, 7 and 8 for the upper rim.

10. Add an extra 15 mm ($\frac{1}{2}$ in) to upper and lower arcs, AJ and CH, to provide the necessary overlap at the join.

11. Cut out the correct shape for the lampshade template.

Calculating the size of the silk and applying the design

Once the template has been made, the silk can be cut and the design drawn larger in pencil on the template. It is a good idea to draw an outline larger than the final lampshade on your silk, 2 cm–3 cm ($\frac{3}{4}$ in–$1\frac{1}{2}$ in). You will paint up to this line so that, should the backing move on application, the colour of the silk will be continuous.

Do not cut out the shaped silk pieces, but pin up and paint as a rectangle. The silk will be trimmed to size later.

Tape the silk carefully into position over your design, (see page 120). Paint as needed, dry and fix. Remove gutta at this stage if necessary. Wash and iron.

Salt and wax textured square lamps with matching cushions ▶

Constructing the lampshade

Equipment: Painted silk
Sticky paper backing
Two rings for top and base
Ruler, tape measure
Pegs
Scissors
Glue or double-sided sellotape
Board

1.   Cut out the sticky backing accurately. Try to make the edges even and smooth.

2.   On a clean, firm surface such as chipboard, stretch out your painted silk. Make sure your work is right side down, i.e. you are looking at the wrong side. You can tape this on the surface or stretch it out using three-pronged pins. (This second method ensures that the silk is perfectly straight and taut.)

Stretched silk pinned upside down; with the backing cut to size for attaching

Lightly glue this edge over to prevent fraying, using a strong rubber-based glue (see below). Trim the other side edge exactly to the backing.

Stretching the silk over the design

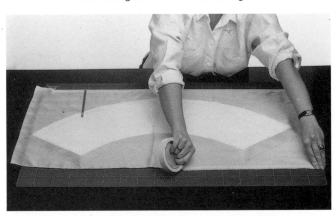

3.   Roll back 5 cm (2 in) of the protective sheet from the backing and position it on the silk. Using smooth, even movements, with your free hand press the backing on to the silk a little at a time. Unroll the backing paper until it is securely attached. There should be no air bubbles if this process is done carefully. Be warned, the backing cannot be removed once it is in position.

4.   Unpin the silk and turn to the right side. Check that all the edges are secured by pressing down with your hands.

5.   Decide which of the two side edges is to be the overlapping one. Using sharp scissors, trim off the surplus silk from this side to 0.5 cm ($\frac{3}{16}$ in) from the edge.

Edges trimmed and glue being applied to top and bottom

6.   Trim the upper and lower longer sides to 1.5–2 cm ($\frac{5}{8}$ in–$\frac{3}{4}$ in). Lightly glue the outside edges of the top and bottom rings. Place to one side. Lightly glue the top and bottom edges only of the lampshade backing. The glue must not touch the silk, but must be clos to the edge. Do not rush; the glue can harden slighty before bonding the rings to the backing.

7.   Starting with the lower ring, roll it carefully along the bottom of the glued backing. Press it against the table as you roll to get a good bonding. Pegs can be placed at intervals to keep it in place. When attaching the square and oval shapes make sure that the centre of your design will be correctly positioned on the ring when assembled. Attach the top ring the same way.

  The conical frame is tricky at this stage, as one ring is much smaller than the other. You may need to peel back the lower ring a little to insert the upper one. Have patience: it will work in the end! Re-glue sections if necessary.

Make sure that the top and bottom edges are aligned before the glue sets, otherwise the back join will look messy.

Rolling the frame on to the sticky backing

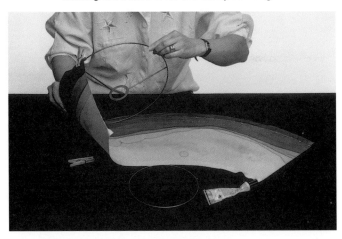

8.   Lightly glue the back edges together with the folded-over side uppermost. Press the glue until set.

9.   Using a blunt screwdriver or fingernail, tuck all the excess silk up under the rim of the ring. Try to do this as neatly and smoothly as possible, as the finish affects the look of your lampshade.

Tucking under the silk to make a neat edge

10.   Assemble your shade with the base or light fitting, and there you are – perfect.

Completed landscape design lampshade and matching cushion

It is possible, instead of using glue, to attach the silk with double-sided tape. This means you replace the glue with tape at each stage. We worry that in the long term the tape will wear and lose its sticking power. The choice, however, is yours; this method is certainly less messy.

PROJECTS

ROSE LAMPSHADE

Material used: 32 cm × 100 cm (13 in × 40 in) crêpe de
Chine
28 cm × 94 cm (11¼ in × 38 in) sticky
backing
94 cm (37½ in) circumference oval rings,
1 top, 1 base
Rubber-based glue
Dimensions: Finished height 28 cm × 94 cm
(11¼ in × 37½ in) length
Technique: Gutta (gold)
Colours: Pink, pale blue, yellow, pale green

1 sq = 1.5 cm

Method

Carefully draw the design on the crêpe de Chine. It is important that the silk is stretched taut and evenly so that when it is mounted the lines in the design remain straight. Position the three roses, one in the centre and two at the sides. Gutta the outlines. When these are dry, paint in the colours. Try to keep them pale but also introduce some careful shading. The roses in particular need this, otherwise they can look rather flat. Fix the silk and complete the lampshade as on pages 120–121.

TULIP LAMPSHADE

Materials: 170 cm × 90 cm (67 in × 36 in) pongée no. 9
160 cm × 90 cm (63 in × 36 in) sticky backing
1 × 25 cm (9¾ in) diameter top ring and bulb support
1 × 50 cm (19¾ in) diameter base ring
rubber glue

Dimensions: Finished height 29 cm (11½ in)
Circumference 160 cm (63 in)

Technique: Gutta, black

Colours: Peach and shades of pale green

1 sq = 1.5 cm

Method

Use the tulip motif at random to create an overall design on the lampshade shape. Gutta the outlines using a large nib so that the black shows up as a clear feature of the design. When dry, paint in the colours. Shading is not necessary but several leaf colours could be used to make the effect more interesting. Fix the silk and complete the lampshade as on pages 120 and 121.

A tulip conical lampshade and matching cushion using black gutta and a stencil tulip cushion

LANDSCAPE LAMPSHADE

See finished design on page 121

Material used: Pongée no. 9 50 cm × 90 cm
(20 in × 36 in)
Rings: top 15 cm (6 in) diameter; base
18 cm (7¼ in) diameter
Sticky backing
Rubber-based glue

Dimensions: Top diameter 18 cm (7 in), base 30 cm
(11¾ in), Height 21 cm (8¼ in)

Colours: Peach, green, cream, grey, navy

Method

The effect of this landscape is achieved by subtle application of dye in the initial stages. Very lightly sketch in hills and sun. Wet the stretched silk with diluent first.

Using cream and palest grey, paint the sky in an arc of these colours. While this is still wet, roll a pale peach colour on a fine brush over the surface. Try to build up cloud forms. Add slightly stronger peach and grey to the base of the clouds. Dry thoroughly.

Paint the hill forms upwards from the base in pale green. Allow the dyes to creep up. Dry quickly once the crinkled effect has been achieved. Paint up from the base again on top of the green using the stronger peach tone; this will now turn more of a brown tone. Dry again when the dye approaches the green. Finally, paint in navy from the base as the last deep colour. Dry thoroughly. Using a cotton bud, dot the surface of the navy dye with alcohol to create an interesting texture. The sun is formed by using alcohol and a cotton bud. Lightly dip the cotton bud into alcohol and a minute amount of navy dye and apply to the silk. Rub carefully from the centre of the sun until a halo of dye is formed on the outside of the circle. Dry quickly once the correct size is achieved.

Complete as described on pages 120 and 121.

ACCESSORIES

GREETINGS CARDS

A hand-painted greetings card is an ideal first project if you are a beginner and reluctant to embark upon something larger. You can try your hand at any one of the silk painting techniques to make your own original card which can be mounted and framed. Bookmarks, postcards, gift tags and notelets can also be made.

A large section of ready-cut mounts and blanks are available with matching envelopes, and it is worth investing in a selection of these for professional looking results. It is quite a simple process to cut your own mounts, however; all you need is the card, a craft knife and a steel ruler.

A selection of pre-cut mounts

Cutting your own mounts

To make your own mount you must choose the paper or card very carefully. If the paper is too thin it will curl and your card will fall down. Card comes in many qualities and textures. Cloud effect, metallic, parchment style, marbled and glossy are all available, so choose one that will complement your silk painting.

Before you decide on the size of your card and cut the paper, make sure you can find an envelope of the appropriate size. Of course, you could make your own envelopes too!

One-fold card

The easiest type to make is from a rectangular piece of card simply folded in half. The silk can be stuck to the front using spray adhesive or bonding web.

A more professional method is to cut a window opening in the front of the card. Different shapes can be cut: squares, rectangles, hearts, or even real window shapes.

One-fold card with window

To work out the size for a one-fold card, measure the size of the silk painting plus a margin of approximately 2 cm ($\frac{3}{4}$ in) all the way around, and then multiply the width by two. Fold the card in half by scoring it lightly on the right side with a craft knife or compass point. You will then obtain a neat, straight fold. On the left-hand side, cut out a window about 1 cm ($\frac{3}{8}$ in) smaller than the silk painting. Cut another piece of card to cover the back.

Two-fold card with window

The card can also be folded into three. This way, the back of the silk can be neatly covered. Decide on the size of your card: it should be the size of the silk painting plus a margin of at least 2 cm ($\frac{3}{4}$ in) all the way around, multiplied by three. The height remains constant. Measuring carefully, divide the card into three. Score the two fold lines on the right side using a craft knife, taking care not to score too hard or you will cut right through the card. In the middle section, cut out the window large enough to display your silk painting, leaving about 1 cm ($\frac{3}{8}$ in) of silk to allow for gluing. Finally, cut a thin strip off from the left side of the card so it will close easily when folded.

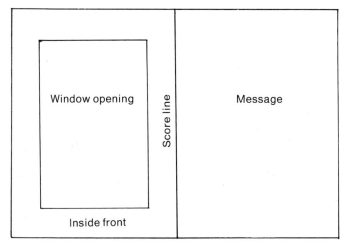

One-fold card

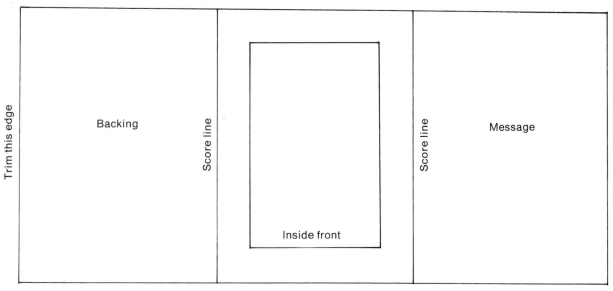

Two-fold card

Mounting your card

There are three different ways of gluing the silk painting into the card: rubber-based glue, spray glue, or bonding web.

Rubber-based glue

A rubber-based glue is the best to use, as any excess can be rubbed off the card when it has dried. With the right side of the silk facing uppermost, glue lightly around the edges of the silk painting. Place the silk face down on the back of the window opening you have cut. Make sure it is in the correct position as it is difficult to re-position it, and take care not to get glue on the front of your card. Wait until the glue is dry before folding the card along the lines you have scored. Sometimes with this method the glue puckers the silk and so if you are using a one-fold window card it is advisable to use another piece of card to cover the back and prevent puckers and bubbles. If you are using a two-fold window card, glue the backing segment (the left-hand side) around the edges and fold over immediately.

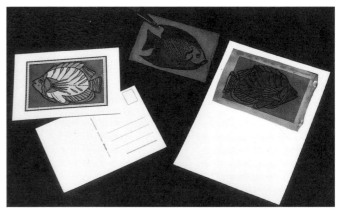

Adhesive-backed postcards

Spray glue

Spray glue is ideal for mounting your cards. Spray the silk and carefully place the painting in the correct position. If you have positioned the silk incorrectly, it can be easily lifted and re-positioned using this adhesive.

If you are using a folded piece of card with no window, you can tear the silk and fray the edges. Lightly spray the card with adhesive and gently place the silk in position.

Glueing silk into a one-fold card

Tearing, fraying and spraying the silk

Flower cards using the salt technique

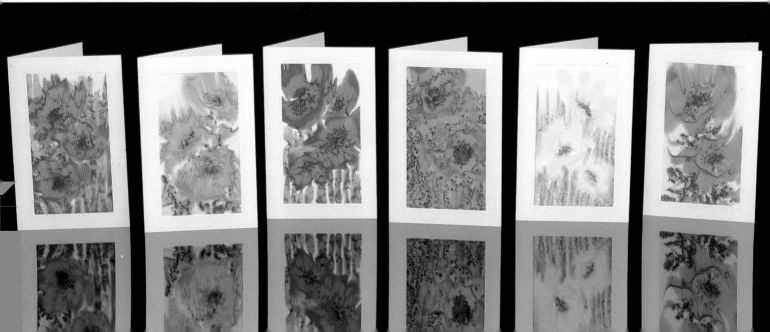

Bonding web

The silk can also be fixed to the card with bonding web. This is a fine mesh of glue with paper stuck to it. The paper is peeled off the glue and it can then be ironed on to your card using a warm dry iron. This is a good way to glue the silk if you do not want a frayed look, as the glue web binds the edges and even enables shapes to be cut.

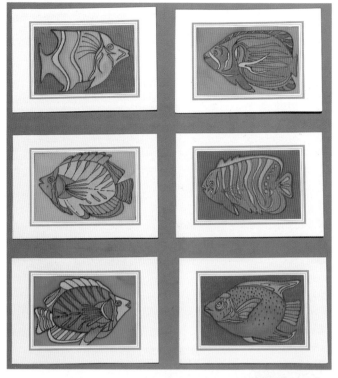

Fish postcards using the gutta technique

A selection of birthday cards, notelets, tags and bookmarks

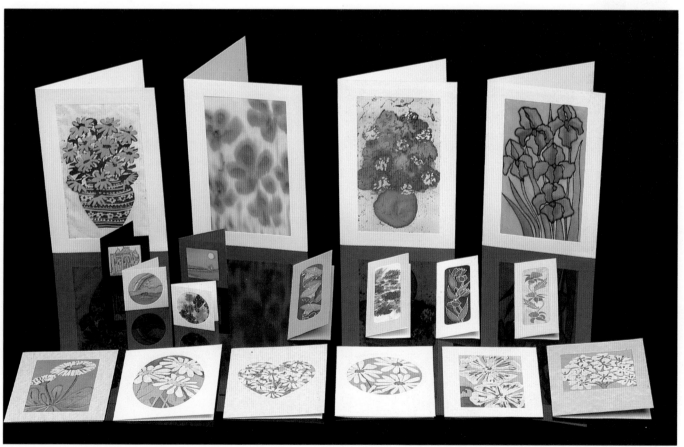

PROJECTS

surface, as the silk should be entirely free from salt before it is fixed. After fixing, cut each painting along the gutta line. Cut mounts and make the cards as shown on page 125.

SALT FLOWER CARDS

See finished designs on page 126

Material used: Silk pongée no. 9
Cards and matching envelopes

Dimensions: Each painting is 10 cm × 18 cm
(4 in × 7¼ in), but it is a good idea to use a larger frame and divide the silk into squares using a gutta line to paint several cards at one time.

Technique: Rock salt

Method

Salt flowers are easy to paint and the results are always different. Individual circles or flowers can be produced by painting the background with water or one colour. Then place a circle of salt crystals on this background and add a few drops of dye to the middle. If you paint the flowers too close together, they will run into each other. You can add a further colour to the centre if desired, and then add stems and leaves. Leave the work in position until it is completely dry, as any movement will spoil the pattern. When it is dry, brush the rock salt from the

WAX DAISY NOTELETS

See finished design on page 127

Material used: Silk pongée no. 9
Notelets and matching envelopes

Dimensions: Each card is 10 cm × 12 cm (4 in × 4¾ in). As you are making a set of 6 notelets, use a large frame and divide the silk into 6 using a wax line.

Technique: False batik

Method

The daisies are painted on the silk using melted wax. Dye is then applied using a large brush. After the silk is dry, repeat the process of waxing and dyeing with each of the colours. When the final colour has dried, remove the wax by ironing the silk between sheets of newsprint with a hot dry iron. Steam or heat fix, depending on the dyes you have used. (See page 24 for more detailed information on false batik.)

After fixing and cleaning, cut the silk into rectangles and mount into the notelets. These can be put into a box and make a wonderful gift.

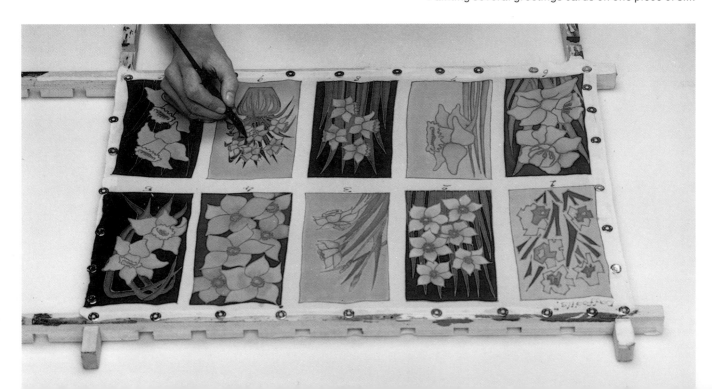

Painting several greetings cards on one piece of silk

1 sq = 1 cm

Use these designs to create your own cards

GUTTA FISH POSTCARDS

See finished designs on page 127

Material used: Silk pongée no. 9
Postcards

Dimensions: Each postcard is 8 cm × 14 cm
($3\frac{1}{4} \times 5\frac{1}{2}$ in). You can paint several cards
on one frame by dividing the silk into
rectangles with gutta

Technique: Gutta (black)

Method

See page 20 for the gutta technique. Use the brightest
dyes you have for these gaily coloured tropical fish. Cut
mounts and make cards as shown on page 125.

BIRTHDAY CARDS

See finished designs on page 127

The stencilling, gutta and wax techniques (see Part Two
of this book) have been used to create these original
cards which your friends will love to receive. Some
diagrams for you to copy are illustrated on page 129. Just
enlarge them to the size you require by using the method
described on page 20.

A display of brooches, earrings and a pendant
The techniques used include salt, salt impregnated
background, wax and antifusant

BROOCHES, PENDANTS, EARRINGS and SCARF CLIPS

The charming pieces of jewellery seen opposite can easily be made to co-ordinate with your outfits. They require such small pieces of silk that any leftover scraps can be used. Why not make earrings to match a silk-painted top or link a scarf clip with a hand-painted silk scarf? A lovely gift idea is a matching card and brooch, ideal for a small birthday present.

A kit for making brooches and the other items is available in some good art and craft shops. It generally consists of a metal front or 'window' with two or three flanges on the side, a convex centre piece of metal over which the silk is stretched and a metal back piece with a fastening for the brooch.

The following description refers to the assembly of a brooch, but also applies to the other items.

When choosing a section of silk to 'frame' in your brooch, look for some interesting effect: maybe a change of colour or a contrast of textures created by wax or antifusant. Place the shape over your silk so that you can see what the finished effect will be through the 'window'.

Equipment for making brooches

A colourful collection of hair accessories. Many silk painting techniques and types of silk are used (see overleaf)

Materials: Small pieces of pongée, crêpe de Chine, soie
sauvage, twill, etc.
Rubber-based glue
Wadding

Method

1.   Choose an interesting piece of your silk. Place the 'window' shape over the area you wish to mount and draw lightly 1 cm ($\frac{3}{8}$ in) away from the shape.

2.   Cut out your silk.

3.   Using a rubber-based glue, lightly coat the surface of the inner rounded metal mount.

4.   Turn the mount upside down and place it on a piece of wadding. Trim around the wadding exactly to the edge of this mount. Leave to dry.

5.   Glue all around the edge of the underside of the mount. Leave for one minute so that the glue will go 'tacky'. Then place the silk on top of the wadding and pull evenly over to the underside of the mount. This should stick into place neatly. Do not pull the silk over too tightly, as it is nice to leave the top side of the brooch slightly rounded.

6.   Place the 'window' over the top of the silk-covered mount and the back fastening section behind. Using a small hammer, tap the small metal fastening keys to hold the brooch together.

The same method of assembling the jewellery applies to the earrings, pendant and scarf clip. If you wish the silk to be flat in your mount, omit the wadding. We have also seen these assembled using double-sided sticky tape on the front and back of the mount as an alternative to glue.

HAIR BANDS, SCRUNCHIES, BOWS and SLIDES

Hair ornaments are an important fashion accessory these days, and can often be rather expensive to buy. If you make your own luxury items, not only will you be wearing an original bow or slide but they will cost very little. All techniques for painting on silk can be used, creating a variety of effects for both day and evening wear.

HAIR BANDS

See finished designs opposite and on page 131
Material used: Soft silk, such as crêpe de Chine or
pongée – cut a strip double the length of
the hair band and the width plus 3 cm
($1\frac{1}{4}$ in)
Hair band

Method

1.   Paint, fix and cut out the strip of silk.

2.   Fold, right sides together, and sew across one end and up one side. Round off the end so that the tip of the hair band will fit in snugly.

3.   Turn through to right side. Feed on to the hair band. Flatten silk for 5 cm (2 in) at the ends, then sew to secure a flat area.

4.   Allow the silk to ruffle and gather across the centre, then flatten at the other end.

5.   Sew up the open end close to the tip. Secure flat area.

SCRUNCHIES

See finished designs below and on page 131
These can be of varying widths and lengths, depending on the effect required when worn. The following instructions are just one suggestion.

Material used: Soft silk, such as crêpe de Chine or pongée. Cut a strip 1.50 m × 25 cm (60 in × 10 in)
Narrow elastic 10–15 cm (4–6 in)

Method

1. Paint, fix and cut out the strip of silk.

2. Fold the silk lengthwise, right sides together, machine the length of strip. Turn through to the right side.

3. Lightly press the seam, but do not flatten the folded edge.

4. Turn in the raw edges 1 cm ($\frac{3}{8}$ in) on one end. Feed the elastic inside the tube and sew very securely across the end.

5. Pull the silk through the tube, gathering up the silk as you pull.

6. Pin this loose elastic to the other end of the scrunchy. Turn under the raw edges and push inside the other, already sewn, end.

7. Trap both ends and elastic with a secure line of machine stitching.

BOWS

Fashion often dictates the size of bows in the hair. Ours are fastened to metallic clips which have two holes at the ends. These enable you to sew the clips securely onto the underside of the bow.

The bows can be made up in many ways. Look at the section on bow ties and see the construction there for the blunt ended method (see page 85). The method is the same, but the measurements were enlarged to suit your finished bow size. The result is rather like the grey and pink bow illustrated on page 131, rather a formal shape.

For the larger bow with pointed ends, simply enlarge the underside and cut diagonal points at the ends. Sew together as for bow tie, omitting, of course, the neckband section.

A pongée silk will probably need stiffening if you are making a large bow. Either an iron-on vilene or cotton would be suitable. If using soie sauvage, there is no need for stiffening.

SLIDES

We were lucky enough to find slide kits in our local craft shop. They are similar to the brooch kits in that they consist of a metal plate, over which the silk is stretched, and a back section which has the metal clip attached.

The method for making up these slides is the same as for the brooches (see opposite). Alternatively, if you can obtain just the metal clips, why not make a long tube of silk and sew it in loops along the length? We show this example in the colour picture on page 131 painted bright turquoise and pink.

A variety of hair accessories using silk painting techniques

Material used : (for large oval box)
Cardboard or pre-cut cardboard kit
Bonding web or glue gun and glue
Scissors, pencil, steel ruler and craft knife
Bonding web 2.50 m (100 in)
Wadding 30 cm × 40 cm (12 in × 16 in)
Painted crêpe de Chine 70 cm (28 in) for outside
80 cm (32 in) pongée no. 9 for lining

Technique

Any of the silk painting techniques can be used to paint the silk used to cover the hat boxes. Opaque gutta on crêpe de Chine and watercolour on wild silk have been used in the picture. Covering the hat boxes inside and outside takes a great deal of painted silk – you may like to use your painted silk on the outside only, and line the box with another material. For best results, we recommend that you use bonding web or a hot glue gun when covering the boxes; however, it is possible to use just fabric glue.

Choose a thicker silk to cover your box, as the thin pongées are too difficult to work with. When you have painted your silk, remember to fix it before covering your hat box.

Method

Hat box kits containing pre-cut cardboard pieces in round, oval and heart shapes are available, but you can cut your own using cardboard, craft knife, scissors and a steel ruler.

1. You will need to cut your card pieces for each hat box: a base, a lid slightly larger than the base, a wide base side and a narrow lid side.

2. If you want to pad the top of your hat box, cut a piece of wadding slightly smaller than the lid.

3. When covering all the pieces of card with your painted silk, the easiest method is to use the iron-on bonding web. A glue gun is also ideal for this. Cover all the pieces of card, clipping the edges of the silk on the round oval or heart-shaped pieces as shown on the photograph frame (see page 136). Glue down carefully. When they are all dry, the lining can be fused in place.

Oval and heart shaped boxes covered in soie sauvage and crêpe de Chine

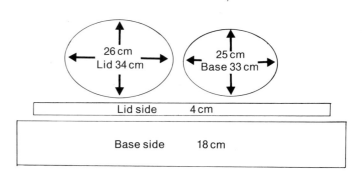

4. Next, working on a flat surface, form the wide base side around the base and mark the overlap with pins or draw a faint pencil line at the top, middle and bottom. Remove the base side and check that the overlap is even all the way down; if it is not, a misshapen box will result.

Equipment needed for covering a hat box

5. Apply glue to the overlap and hold together until dry. Glue the base into the bottom of the shaped base side. Continue by repeating the same process with the lid and lid side. Make sure that the overlap line matches the overlap line on the base.

6. Piping, cording, ribbons, tassels, etc. can be used to finish off your hat box.

PHOTO FRAMES

Material used: Mount board or old used photograph
frame
Wadding
Glue
Painted silk
Scissors, pencil, steel ruler, craft knife

Technique

Any of the silk painting techniques can be used to paint the silk needed to cover the photograph frame. Gold gutta, salt, watercolour and wax techniques have all been used in the photograh shown on below.

A selection of silk covered photograph frames using salt, gutta and wax techniques

Method

It may be possible to buy pre-cut mount board photograph frame kits at your craft shop. If not you can easily cut your own from mount board using a craft knife and a steel ruler, or find an old cardboard photograph frame which you can cover.

1.   First of all you must work out how much silk you will need to paint. This will depend, of course, on the size of photograph frame you wish to cover. If you intend to cover both sides of the back board and make a stand, you will need approximately four times the size of the back board plus 5 cm (2 in) all around. However, twice the size of the mount plus 5 cm (2 in) all around is enough for a frame with no stand. Remember to fix the silk before starting to cover the frame.

2.   Before cutting and gluing the silk, measure and cut the wadding. Cut the wadding 0.25 cm ($\frac{1}{8}$ in) smaller than the outside measurement of the frame. Trace the opening shape on the wadding and cut it out.

3.   To cover the front board of the frame, cut the silk 5 cm (2 in) larger on all sides of the board. Place the board in the middle on the wrong side of the silk. Trace around the oval, round or rectangular opening. Draw another line 2 cm ($\frac{3}{4}$ in) inside the first line. Cut out the shape on the second line.

4.   Place the cardboard mount on top of the silk using the traced line as a guide. Clip the curves as shown in the diagram, fold them over and glue. Continue around the opening until all the edges are glued.

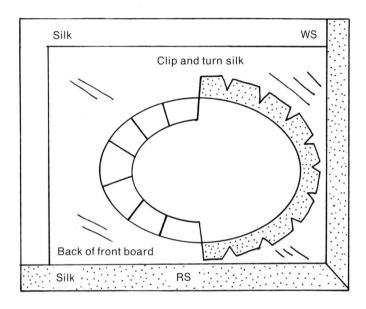

5.   If you have decided to pad your photograph frame, now is the time to add the wadding. When the glue is dry, turn over the board, lift up the silk and put the wadding down on the board. Lay the silk evenly over the wadding and turn the board over. Spread glue along the edges of the back of the card and fold the silk around it, making sure that the corners are finished with a neat tuck. If you have an oval or round frame, clip the edge of the silk as you did for the window opening.

6.   The back board can now be covered in the same way as the outer edge of the front board. Both sides of the back board can be covered if you wish.

A stand can be covered with silk and glued on to the back of the frame if you plan for the photograph to stand on a table. The back and front boards are now ready to be glued together, leaving enough space to slip your photograph into the frame.

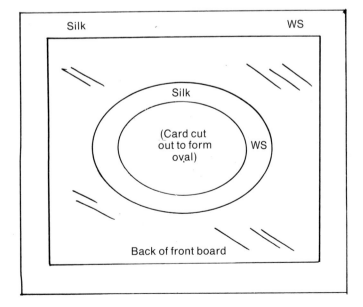

COATHANGERS, POMANDERS, LAVENDER BAGS and TISSUE HOLDERS

These small items will take almost no time to make up and require very little silk. They look so attractive, you will not only want to give them as gifts but also to use them to ornament your own bathroom and dressing room. Your finest evening wear can be hung on matching padded coathangers and the pot pourri in the pomanders will freshen up a toilet or stuffy wardrobe. Lavender sachets in drawers will keep your clothes fresh.

Once you start, you will find it difficult not to continue producing small decorative items from leftover scraps of silk. Some can be made without a sewing machine.

Any silk painting technique can be used to colour your silk. Often the colours themselves are very pretty, so a lot of time spent on detailed work is not necessary. Salt impregnated background flowers, sea salt on toning colours, or background colour washes with dots of colour on the top could all make interesting textures.

COATHANGER

See finished designs on page 138
Material used: A good quality wooden coathanger
Wadding
Painted crêpe de Chine 15 cm (6 in) wide × 3 cm (1$\frac{3}{16}$ in) longer than hanger
Matching narrow ribbon
Fake silk flower
Rubber-based glue

Method

1. Wind the wadding evenly around the coathanger until it is 15 cm (6 in) in circumference. Make sure that the ends are covered well.

2. Using ribbon, cover the coathanger hook. A dot of glue will hold the ribbon to the end while you wind downwards. Towards the base, tuck in a pretty silk flower and secure by winding further over it to the base of the wire. Glue carefully and securely.

3. Cut out the rectangle of silk 15 cm (6 in) wide and 3 cm (1$\frac{3}{16}$ in) longer than the wooden hanger. Iron inwards turnings of 1 cm ($\frac{3}{8}$ in) on all four sides.

4. Pin the folded edges together over the top of the squashy wadding. Tack carefully, making sure that the ends are nicely rounded.

5. Using a matching thread, neatly oversew the length of the seam. An alternative is to use little running stitches, although oversewing is neater.

POMANDER

See finished design on page 138
Material used: Painted silk, pongée or crêpe de Chine 24 cm (9$\frac{1}{2}$ in) diameter
Circle of wadding 18 cm (7$\frac{1}{4}$ in) diameter
Handful of pot pourri
1.5 m (60 in) narrow satin ribbon
1 m (40 in) decorative lace
Pretty silk flower

Method

1. Draw a large circle, 24 cm (9$\frac{1}{2}$ in) diameter or large dinner plate size, on the silk.

2. Zigzag the lace to the outside edge of the silk circle. (This stage could be hand sewn).

3. Cut out a smaller circle of wadding and place in the centre of the circle. Place a handful of pot pourri on top.

4. Gather up the circle of silk and tie the ribbon firmly round to form a ball shape. The pomander will need a hanging loop and a bow.

5. Before tightening the ribbon, slip a flower into the middle of the pomander. Trim the ribbon ends diagonally.

LAVENDER BAGS

Lavender can be put into any shaped sachet of silk and tied with pretty satin ribbon. This design looks attractive using salted silk and a pretty edging of automatic machine embroidery pattern.

Material used: Pongée or crêpe de Chine 26 cm × 13 cm (10½ in × 5¼ in)
Matching thread
Satin ribbon for bow
Dried lavender

Method

1. Cut out two circles of silk approximately 12–13 cm (5–5¼ in) across. Draw on a centre circle of 8 cm (3¼ in) across using a fade-away marker pen.

2. Pin the two pieces together. Set the machine stitch to satin stitch zigzag. Join the two pieces together on the centre circle line, leaving a small gap.

3. Firmly stuff the centre with lavender, then zigzag over the opening to seal the lavender in.

4. Set the machine stitch to automatic scallop design. Zigzag over the outside circle line in the scallop pattern. Using sharp, pointed scissors cut round the edge close to the scallop to show a pretty edge.

5. Sew a satin ribbon in the centre bow to decorate.

TISSUE HOLDER

Material used: Rectangular piece of painted silk
Plain white silk for the lining
Wadding
Lace for the edging

Method

1. Cut out one rectangle each of painted silk, plain silk and wadding. These should all be the same size. The rectangle needs to be the length of the bought tissue packet plus 3 cm (1³⁄₁₆ in). The width of the rectangle is double the width of the packet plus 3 cm (1¹⁄₁₆ in).

2. The finished design has two bands of lace on the inside edge. Cut two pieces of lace the same length as the tissue packet, plus 3 cm (1¼ in). Place the layers on the table: wadding, painted silk, lace (frilled edges towards the centre) and plain silk on the top.

3. Machine down the two shorter sides, catching the lace in the middle. Turn through to the right side.

4. Place on the table with the lace and painted silk uppermost. Fold the two lace edges to meet in the centre. Machine and neaten across the ends.

Pretty covered coathangers, pomanders, lavender bags and a tissue holder

CHRISTMAS STOCKINGS, TREE DECORATIONS and CARDS

CHRISTMAS STOCKINGS

Finished size: 25 cm × 40 cm (10 in × 16 in)
Material used: Two pieces painted pongée no. 9
30 cm × 45 cm (12 in × 18 in)
Two pieces cotton or silk lining
30 cm × 45 cm (12 in × 18 in)
2 pieces wadding 30 cm × 45 cm
(12 in × 18 in)
Red loop for hanging
Technique: Gutta (gold)
Colours: Red, green

Method

1. Gutta the motifs across the silk, putting the name at the top and continuing downwards in bands of varying widths.

2. Paint alternate rows in reds and greens.

3. Fix as normal.

Sewing up

1. Make a cardboard template of the stocking shape plus 1.5 cm ($\frac{5}{8}$ in) turnings.

2. Draw round the template on the painted silk and cotton lining. Cut out a pair of each. Cut out one pair in wadding without the seam allowance.

3. Pin, right sides together, the top of the stocking front and back to their cotton linings. Tack, machine and turn over so that the right sides are uppermost.

4. Place the wadding between the stocking front and back sections.

5. Pin and tack the front stocking to the back stocking section, right sides together. Machine around the leg and toe. Zigzag the edge to neaten. Clip at the corners.

6. Turn through to the right side and press.

7. Sew on hanging loop in top right-hand corner.

Bright cards, tags and Christmas stockings

Unusual tree decorations, baubles and angels

139

CHRISTMAS CARDS and GIFT TAGS

See finished designs on page 139
See details on how to make cards on page 125. Look at old cards for design ideas – Christmas trees, angels, doves, baubles, presents, robins, snow scenes, poinsettias, bells; all could be utilized for your personal cards.

Any of the silk painting techniques could be used: gutta, watercolour, stencilling, spraying, wax and salt.

TREE BAUBLES

See finished designs on page 139
These perspex tree decorations are great fun to make. They depend on the availability of the round and heart-shaped decorations in your craft shops. It is easiest to paint a few at a time on one square of silk. Each bauble only needs a circle approximately 10 cm (4 in) of silk.

Material used: Perspex shapes – ball or heart
Dimensions: Small square of silk 45 cm × 45 cm (18 in × 18 in) (8 balls)
Transparent glue
Gold or coloured braid
Cord for hanging
Technique: Gutta (gold or black)

Method
Draw around the half globe or heart to obtain the correct size. Your design must fit neatly into this shape. Gutta and paint the designs. Try to use concentrated dye, so that the colours are strong and bright when fixed.

Assembling your shape

1. Using sharp pointed scissors, cut neatly around the shape allowing 0.5 cm ($\frac{3}{16}$ in) extra for joining.

2. Glue the rim of one half of the shape using a transparent glue. Place the trimmed silk on top and allow to dry. Press lightly with your hand to make sure it is in contact with the edge.

3. Push the other half of the shape over the first to seal together. Carefully match up the hole at the top.

4. Glue lightly around this join and disguise it using a narrow gold or coloured braid.

5. Attach a loop through the top and your decoration is ready for display.

PADDED GOLD ANGELS

See finished designs on page 139
These three-dimensional silk angels are effective as a group display. Design them so that each one is in a different position. They need to be sewn and padded, so their outline must be easy to machine around.

Material used: For eight angels you will need approximately 90 cm × 40 cm (36 in × 16 in) pongée no. 9
Cotton lining fabric of a similar size
Wadding
Gold card for hanging
Technique: Gutta (gold)

Method
Draw out matching back and front designs on the silk using the designs opposite. Our angels are about 10–12 cm (4–5 in) finished height. Use gold gutta for the outlines and paint in the angels using shades of yellow and brown dye. The shading is very important on these pieces to add visual interest.

Assembly

1. Cut out round your angel shape leaving a 1 cm ($\frac{3}{8}$ in) seam allowance. Cut out a matching lining for both the front and back in cotton.

2. Tack the front and back to their lining pieces.

3. Pin right sides together; machine around the angel shape. Leave a gap on straight section for turning.

4. Clip and trim carefully and turn through to the right side. Press.

5. Pad the angel using a small amount of wadding at a time and push into place using a knitting needle. Oversew the opening neatly together.

6. Attach a small gold loop of card to the top of each angel ready for hanging.

Use these designs on your Christmas projects, or create your own using old cards for ideas   **1 sq = 1 cm**

GLOSSARY

All-over design A design that is repeated throughout a piece of work.

Antifusant Also known as stop-flow or antispread, this is a liquid which controls the flow of the dyes on the surface of the silk and allows detailed work.

Appliqué Pieces of fabric applied to a background fabric and held down by stitching.

Appliqué (trapunto) Raised appliqué work. After machining the back fabric is slit and stuffed with wadding.

Bias Strip or binding – a piece of fabric cut across the grain.

Brads Metal insertions used in picture framing.

Cut-out The piece of card which is removed when a window is cut in the matt board.

Diffuser A metal gadget used to spray dye on to the silk. Air is blown through the mouthpiece.

Diluent This can be used instead of the 50/50 alcohol/water solution for diluting the dyes. Helps to prevent streaking.

Epaississant Also known as thickener; can be mixed with the dyes to form a paste-like substance to enable direct painting on to the silk.

'Free embroidery' Fabric is stretched on an embroidery frame. The design is executed using a sewing machine set in darning position.

Gutta – serti An opaque, colourless, rubber-based resist. This is used to block the silk and control the flow of the dyes.

Gutta – solvent This is used to change the consistency of the gutta. It is also used to clean nibs when they become blocked with gutta.

Grain The direction of the fabric threads. The yarns run parallel to the selvages forming the lengthwise grain. Silk can easily be torn across the grain. Paper sometimes has a visible grain.

Lining A cotton or nylon fabric used for backing.

Matt Also known as mount or passe partout, a protective board to cover the painting with a window cut in it for viewing.

Matt board A multi-ply paper board from which mounts are made. It is available in many colours, grades and textures.

Mitre The angle on which the corner of the frame is cut.

Motif A feature of a design or pattern which is either the central point of attention or is used repeatedly throughout the design.

Nib The metal-tipped applicator for the gutta, also known as the nomographic nib.

Pantograph A tool to enable the enlargement or reduction of a drawing.

Perspex Clear plastic used instead of glass on the front of pictures.

Piping A fold of bias fabric covering a cord giving a tailored edge to a piece of work in matching or contrasting fabric.

Presser foot Standard foot for normal sewing on a machine.

Quilting The process of joining two or more layers of material together with a decorative stitch.

Italian: cord inserted between parallel lines of stitching.

Trapunto: *see appliqué*

Rings Metal hoops used for lampshade making.

Resist *see gutta or wax*

Slip stitch Tiny hand stitches taken through and under a fold of fabric where the stitching must be invisible.

Velcro A trade name for a fastening strip made in two sections, one with a velvet finish, the other a hooked surface, which adhere when the sections are pressed together.

Wadding Thick wool or terylene fabric, used as the middle layer between the silk and the backing when quilting. Adds warmth and 'body' to a garment.

Wax A resist on silk. Stops the dye from spreading.

SUPPLIERS

Britain

Painting on Silk
22 Wainwright Road
Altrincham
Cheshire WA14 4BW

Pongées Ltd
184–186 Old Street
London EC1V 9BP

Wm H. Bennett & Sons Ltd
Crown Royal Park
Higher Hillgate
Stockport SK1 3HB

Dryad Ltd
P.O. Box 38
Northgates
Leicester LEI 9BU

E. J. Arnold & Sons Ltd
Parkside Lane
Densbury Road
Leeds LS11 5TD

Candle Makers Suppliers
28 Blythe Road
London W14 0HA

Atlantis Paper Company Ltd
Gullivers Wharf
105 Wapping Lane
London E19 RW

L. Cornellissen & Son Ltd
105 Great Russell Street
London WC1

George Weil & Sons Ltd
18 Hanson St
London W1P 7DB

Craft Creations Ltd
1–4 Harpers Yard
Ruskin Road
Tottenham
London N1Z PNC

Europe

Sennelier
Rue du Moulin à Cailloux
Orly, Senia 40894567
France

R. Leprince
19 rue de Cléry
75002 Paris
France

Ponsart Frères
28 rue du Sentier
75002 Paris
France

Pébéo, Usine St Marcel
13367 Marseille
France

Dupont
route de Guindreef
44600 Saint-Nazaire
France

La Fourmi 211
rue Vanderkindere

1180 Brussels
Belgium

Le Folio
Paris St Henri 56
1200 Brussels
Belgium

Passe Temps
Avenue Georges Henri 292
1200 Brussels
Belgium

Galerie Smend
Mainzer Strasse 28
Postfach 250450
0–5001 Köln 1
West Germany

Hobbidee
Turbinstrasse 7
7600 Stuttgart 31
West Germany

USA

Artis Inc.
Box 407
Sovang
CA 93463

Batik Art Place
410 Boas Dr
Santa Rosa
CA 94505

Cerulean Blue Ltd
P.O. Box 21168

Seattle
WA 98111

Colorcraft Ltd
P.O. Box 936
Avon
CT 06001

Ivy Crafts Imports
5410 Annapolis Rd
Bladensburg
MD 20710

Oriental Silk Co.
8377 Beverly Blvd
Los Angeles
CA 90048

Savoie Faire
3020 Bridgeway Suite
305
Sansalito
CA 94965

Straw into Gold
3006 San Pablo St
Berkley
CA 94702

Thai Silks
252 State St
Los Altos
CA 94022

Screwary Trading Ent
111 Peter St; Suite 211
Toronto
Ontario MSV ZH1
Canada

INDEX